Insiders

30 Pictures ready to color

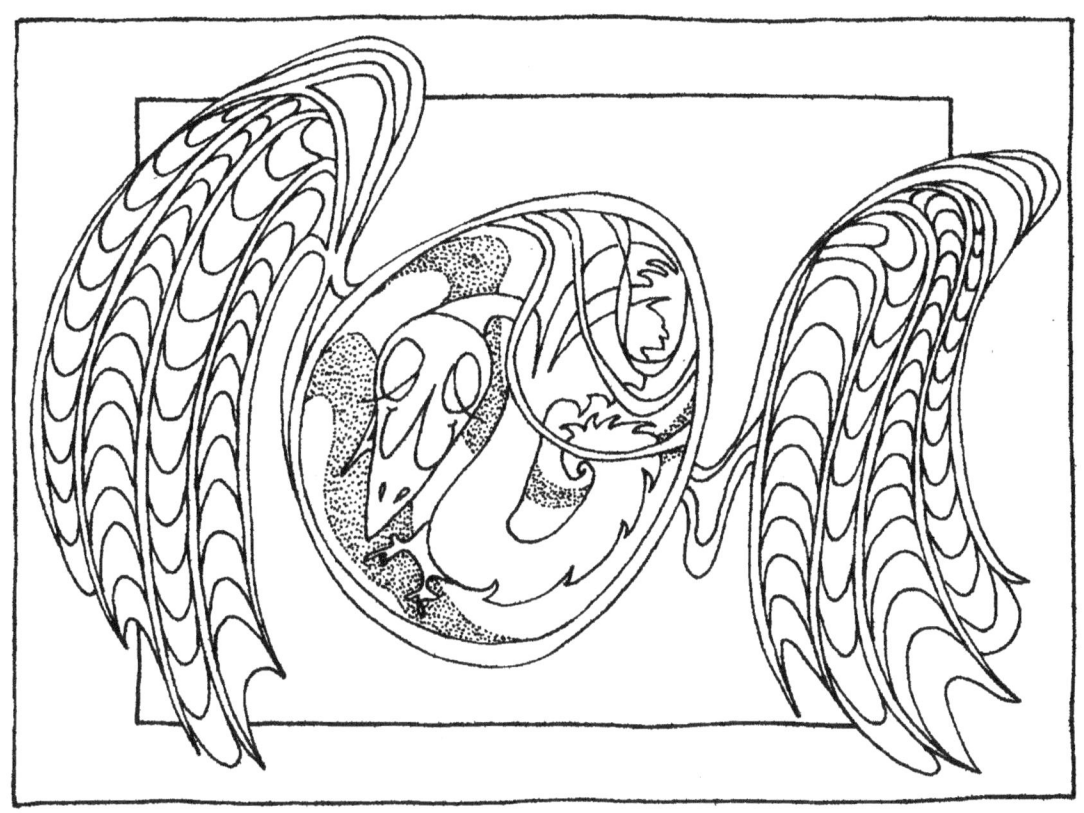

©2018 Joan Worth
De Pere, Wisconsin
ALL RIGHTS RESERVED
ISBN-13: 978-1719055611
ISBN-10: 1719055610

INSIDERS ©2018 Joan Worth De Pere, Wisconsin

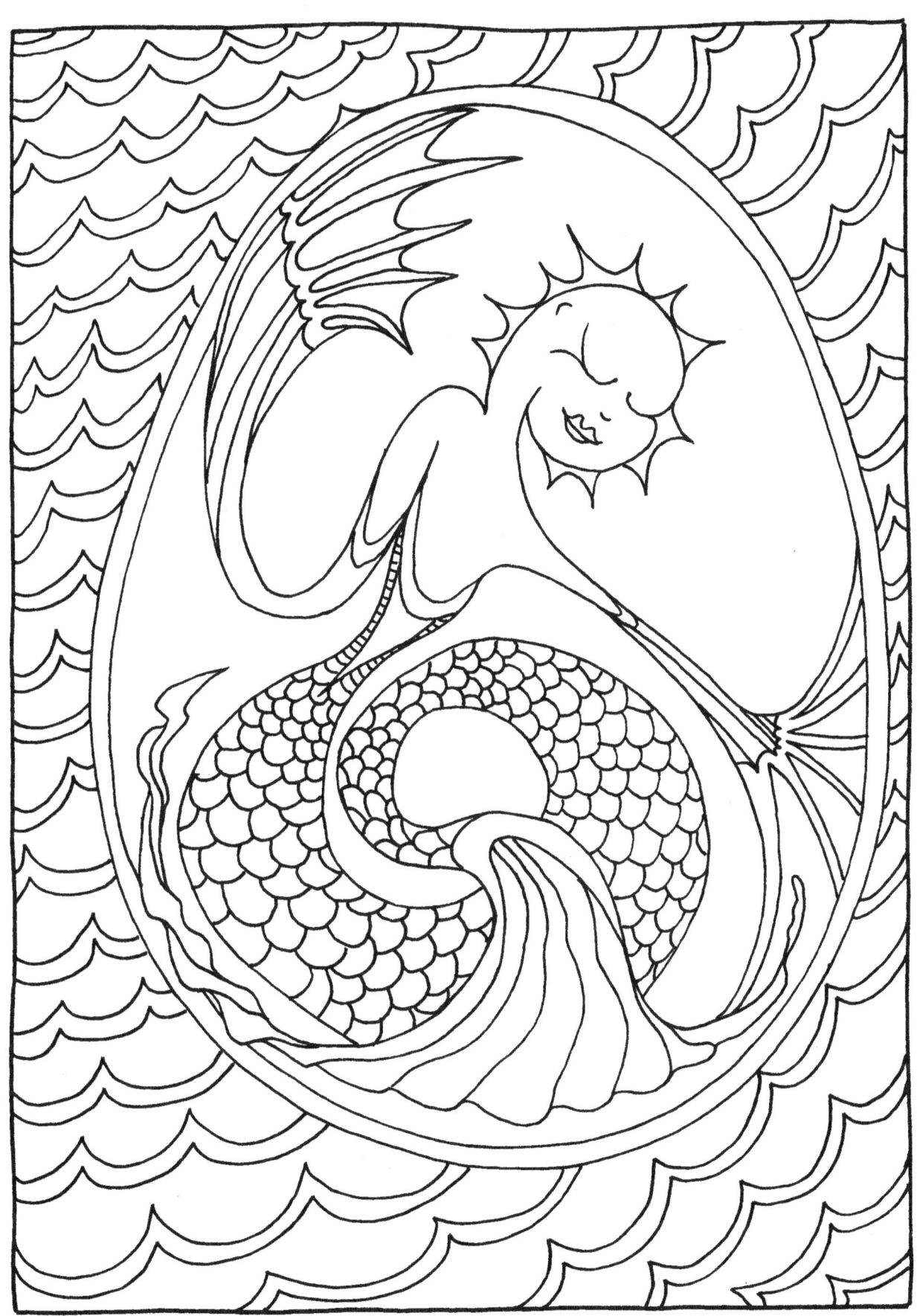

INSIDERS ©2018 Joan Worth De Pere, Wisconsin

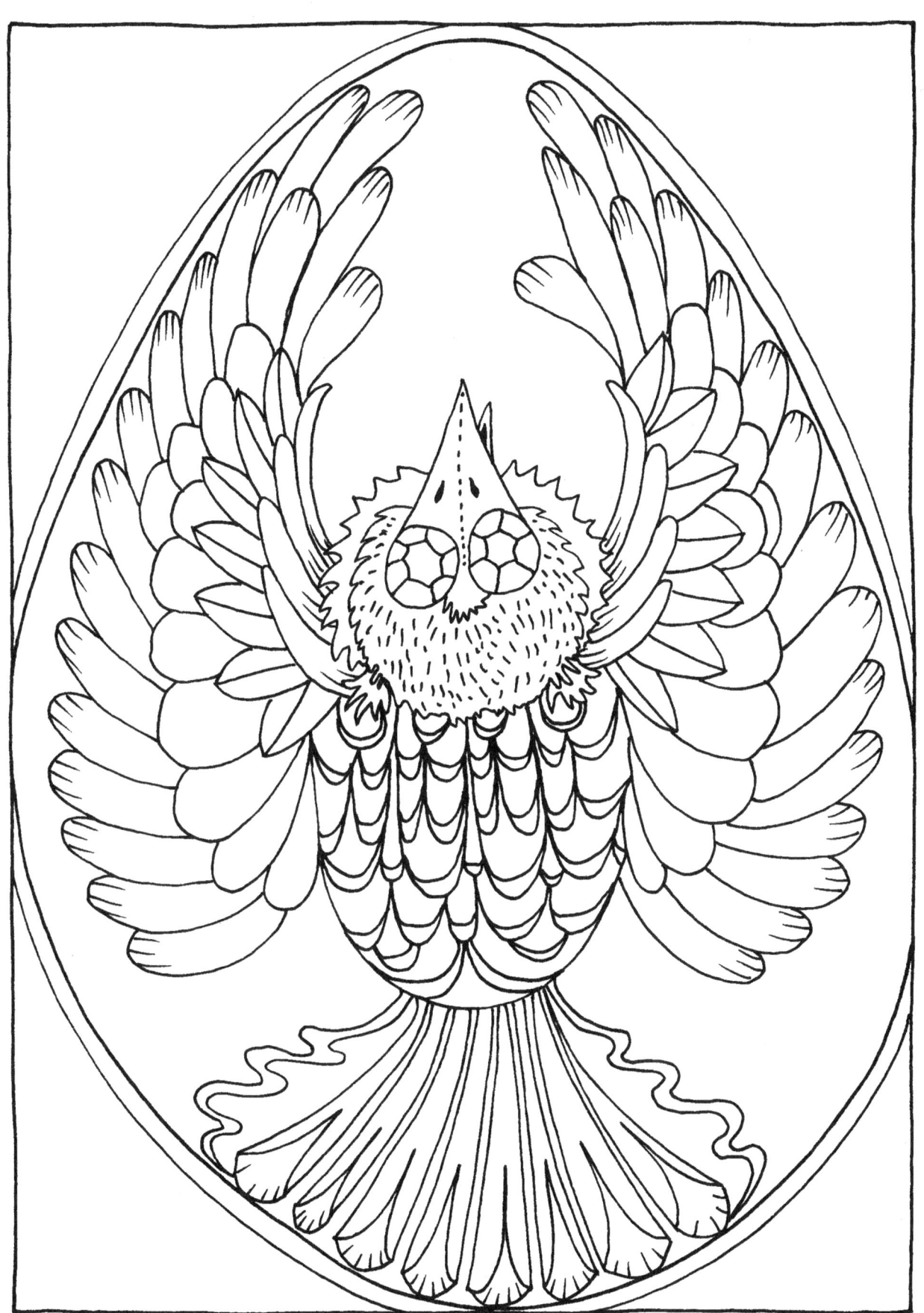

INSIDERS ©2018 Joan Worth De Pere, Wisconsin

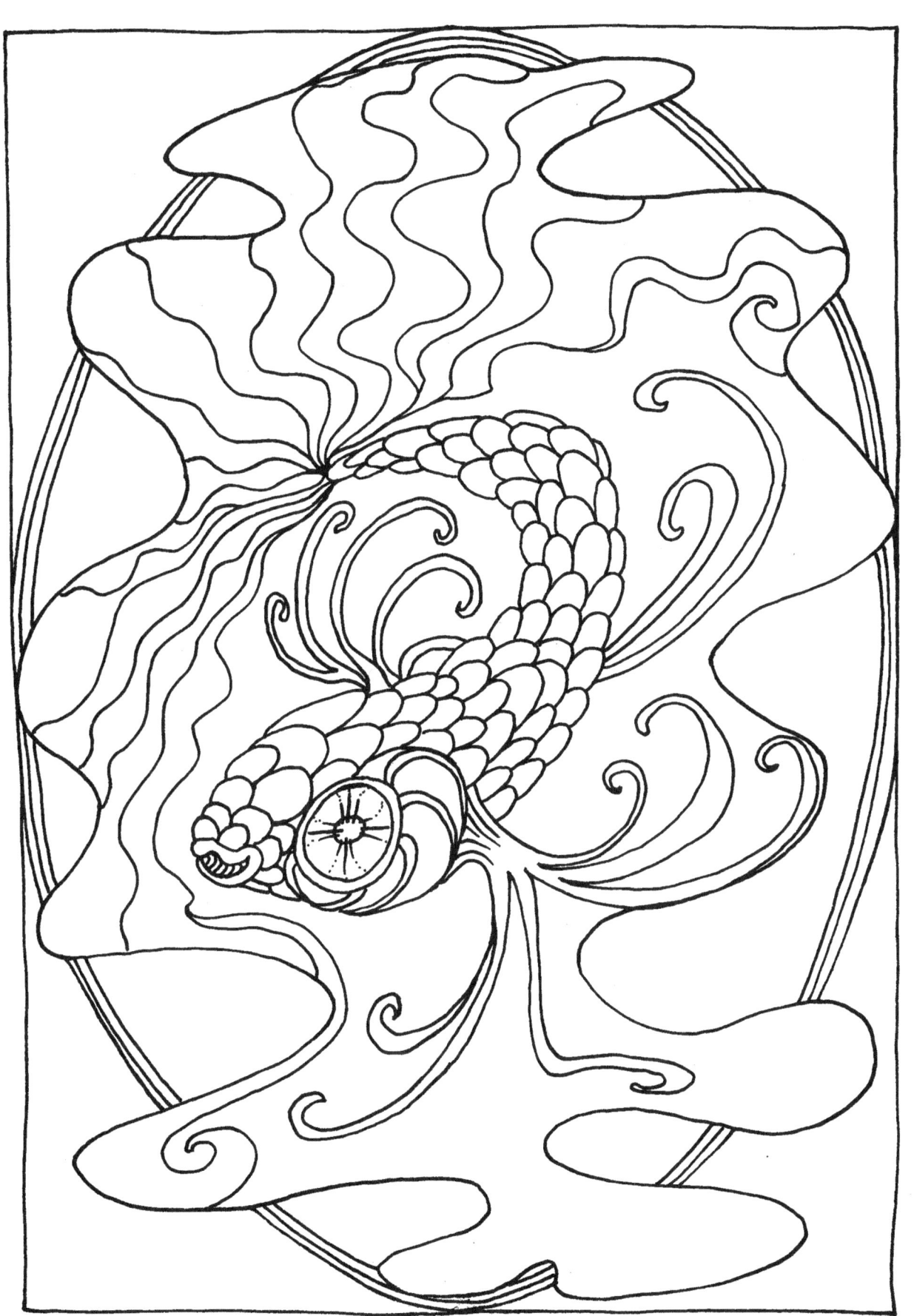

INSIDERS ©2018 Joan Worth De Pere, Wisconsin

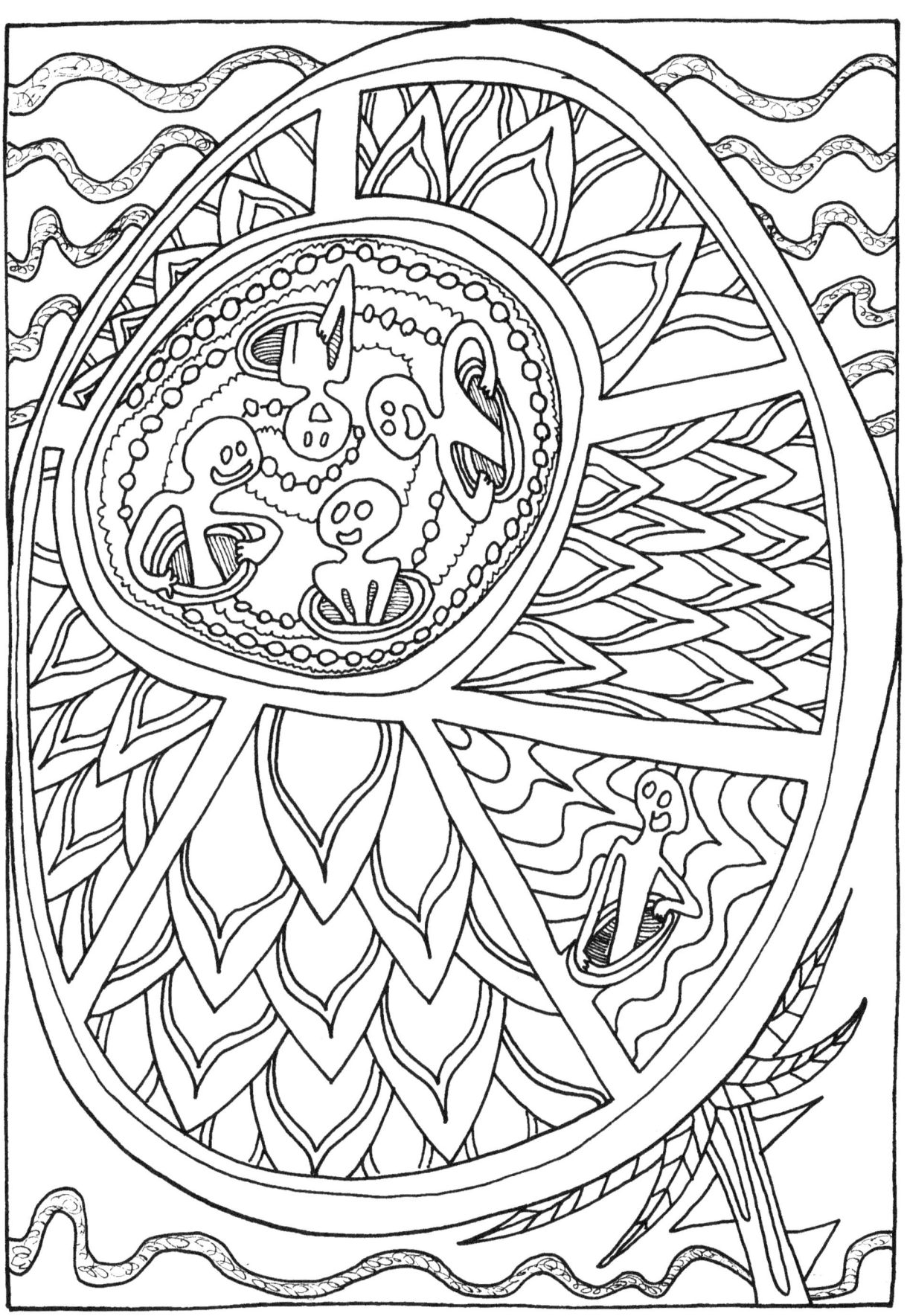

INSIDERS ©2018 Joan Worth De Pere, Wisconsin

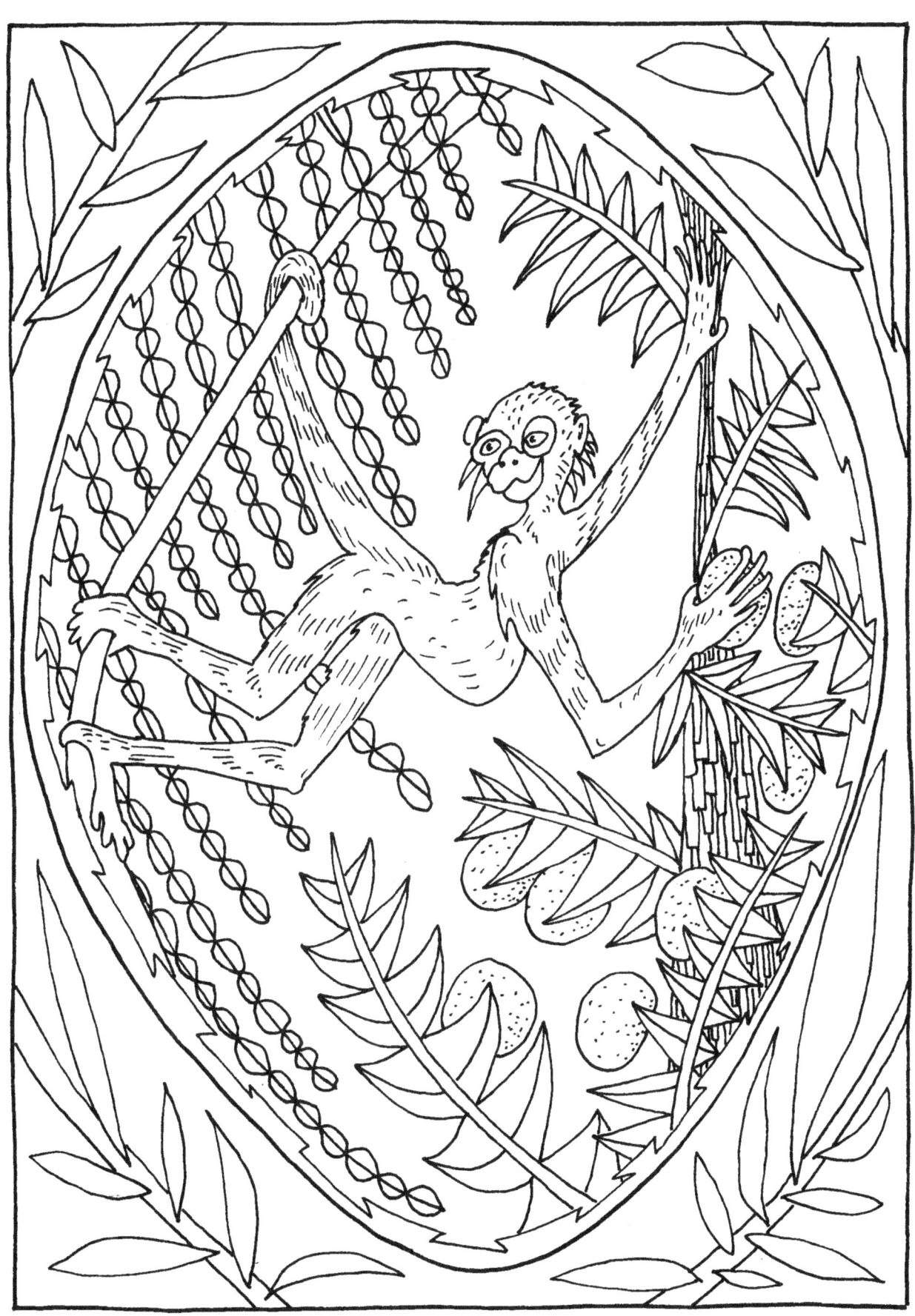

INSIDERS ©2018 Joan Worth De Pere, Wisconsin

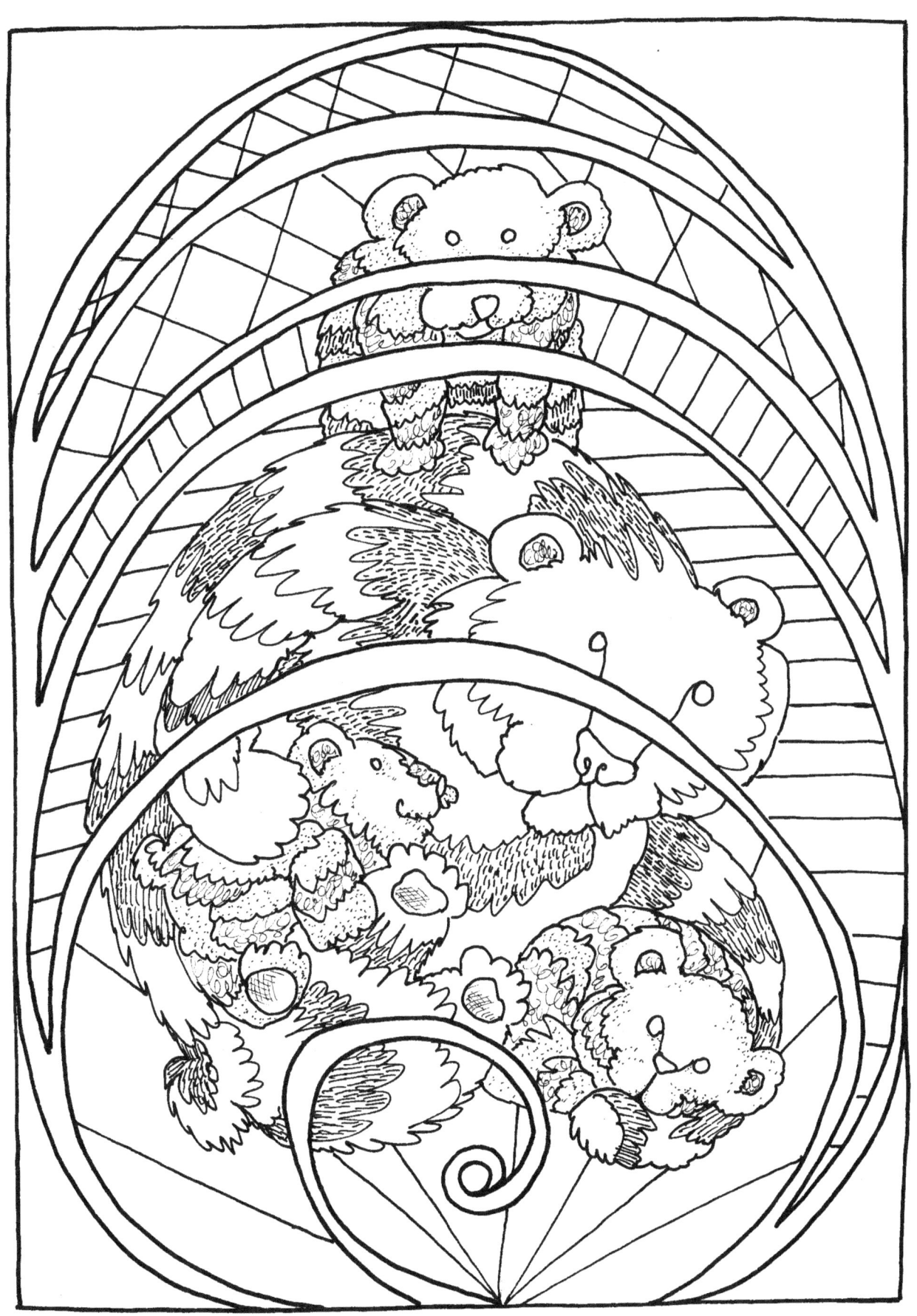

INSIDERS ©2018 Joan Worth De Pere, Wisconsin

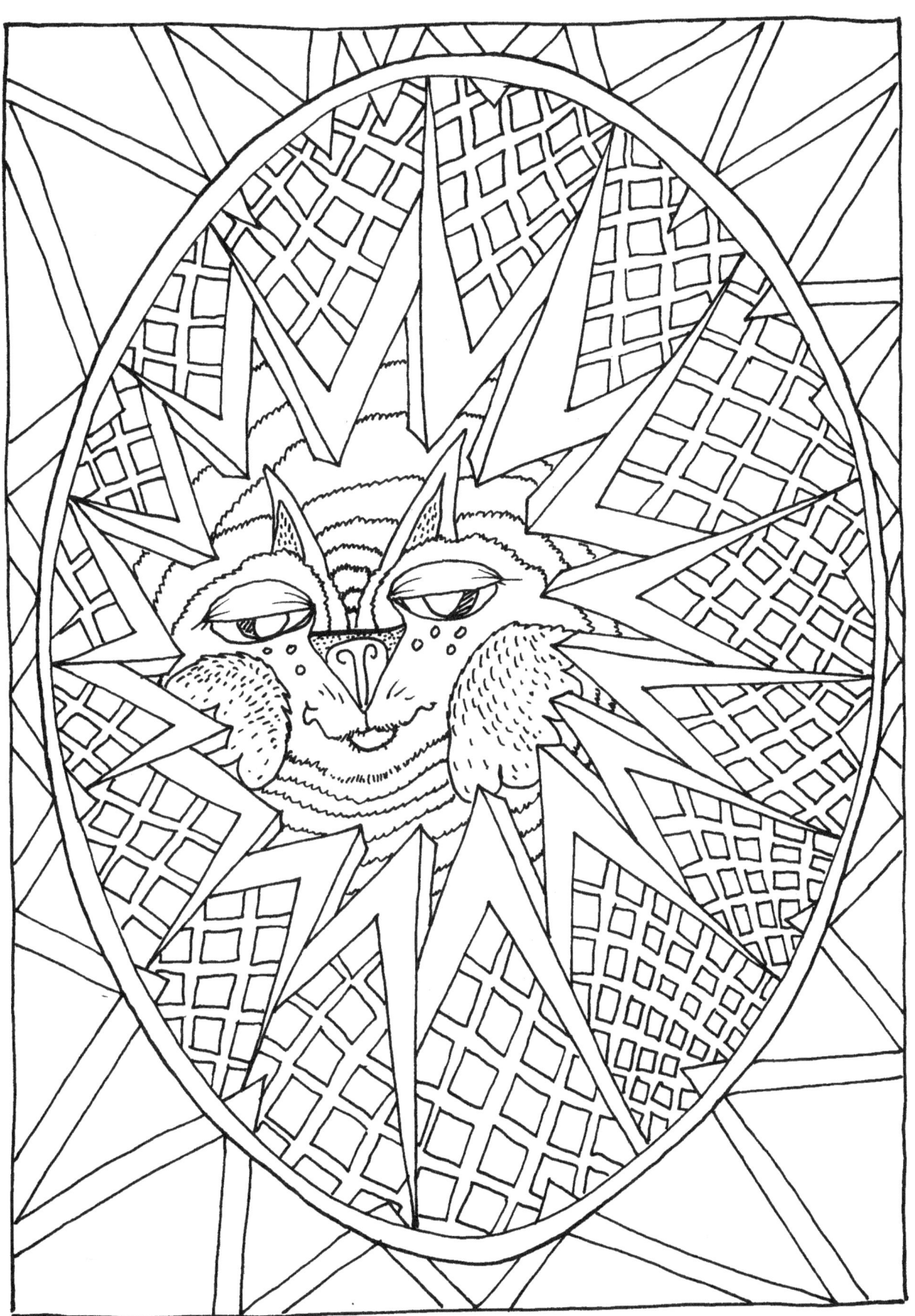

INSIDERS ©2018 Joan Worth De Pere, Wisconsin

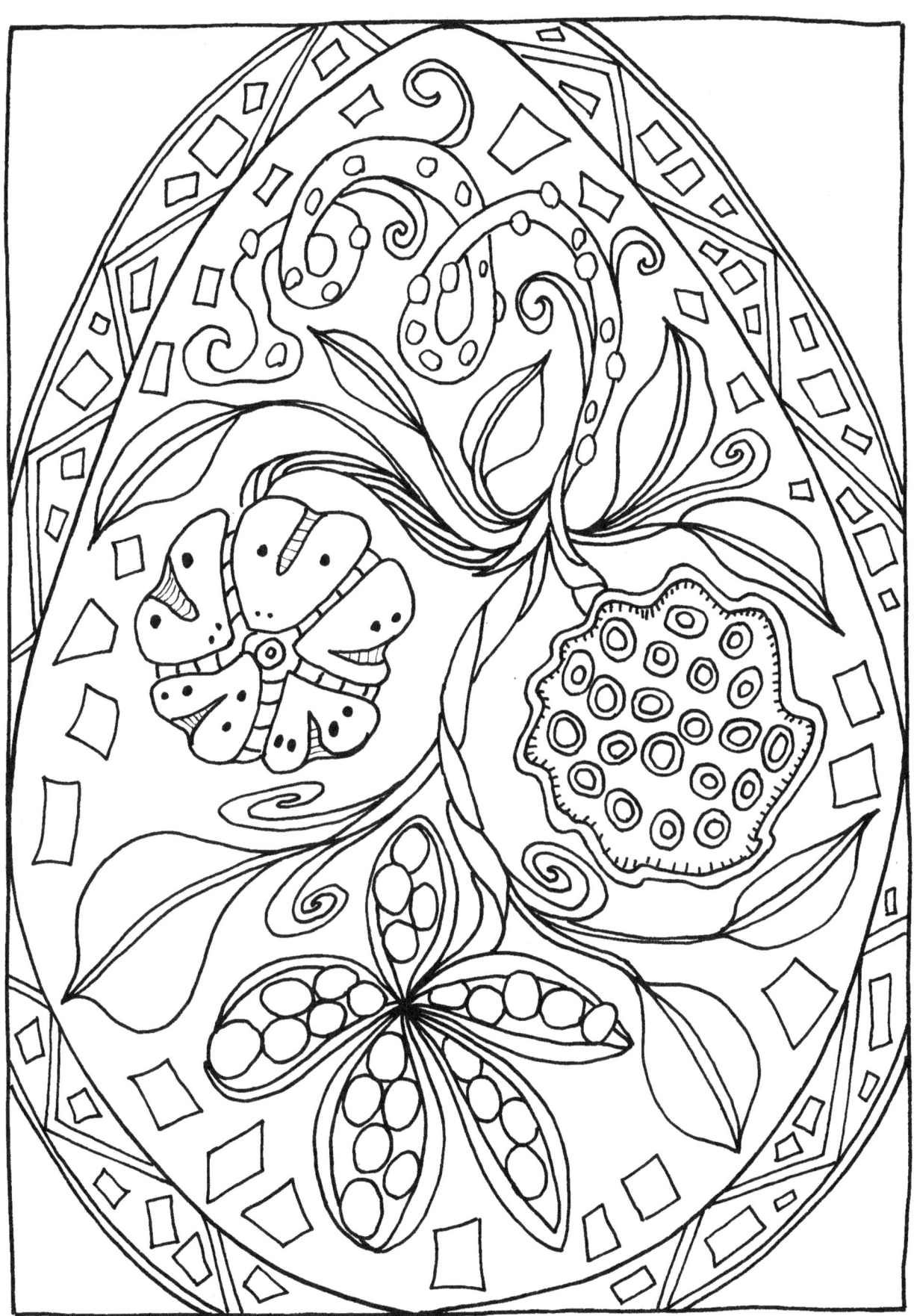

INSIDERS ©2018 Joan Worth De Pere, Wisconsin

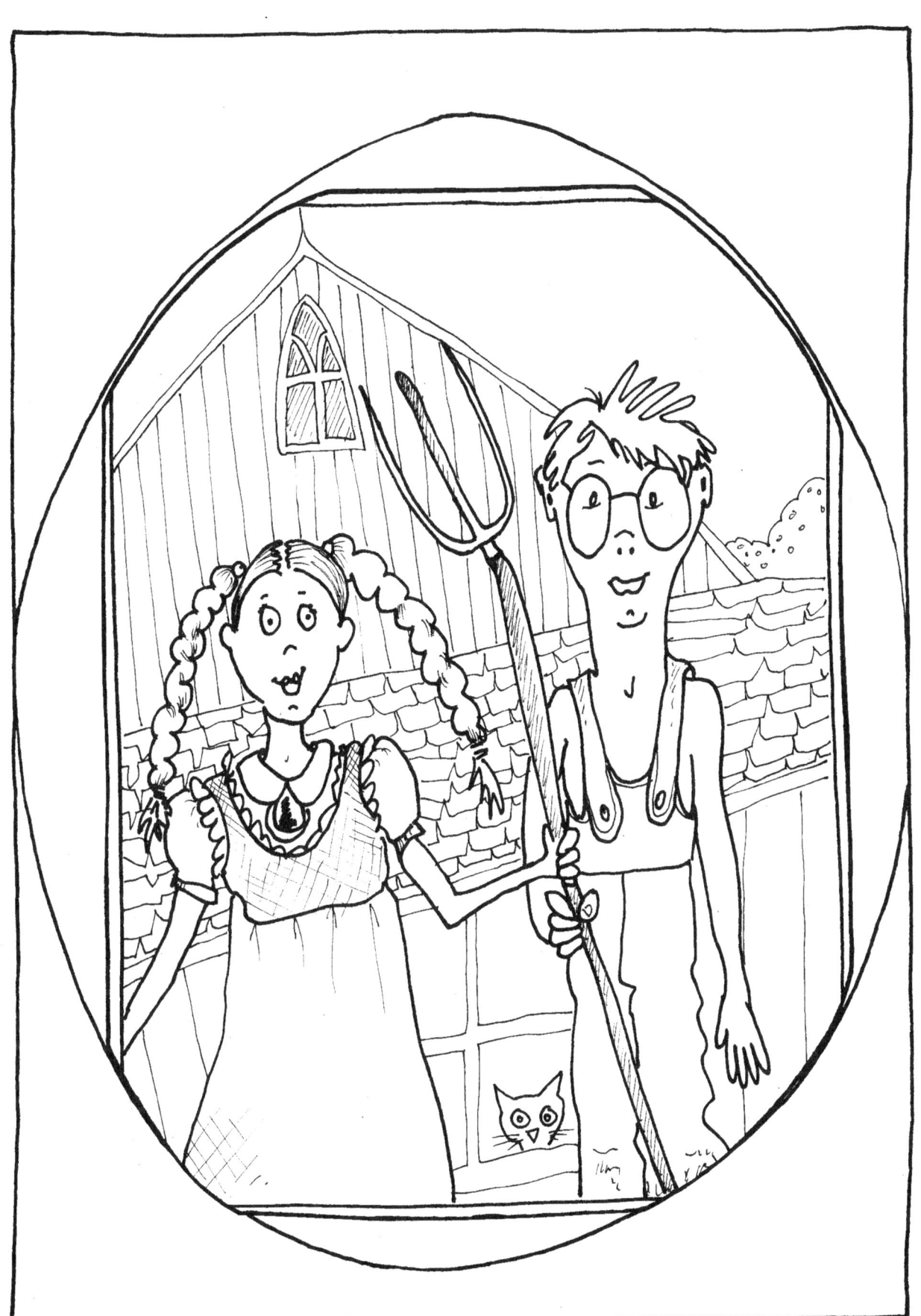

INSIDERS ©2018 Joan Worth De Pere, Wisconsin

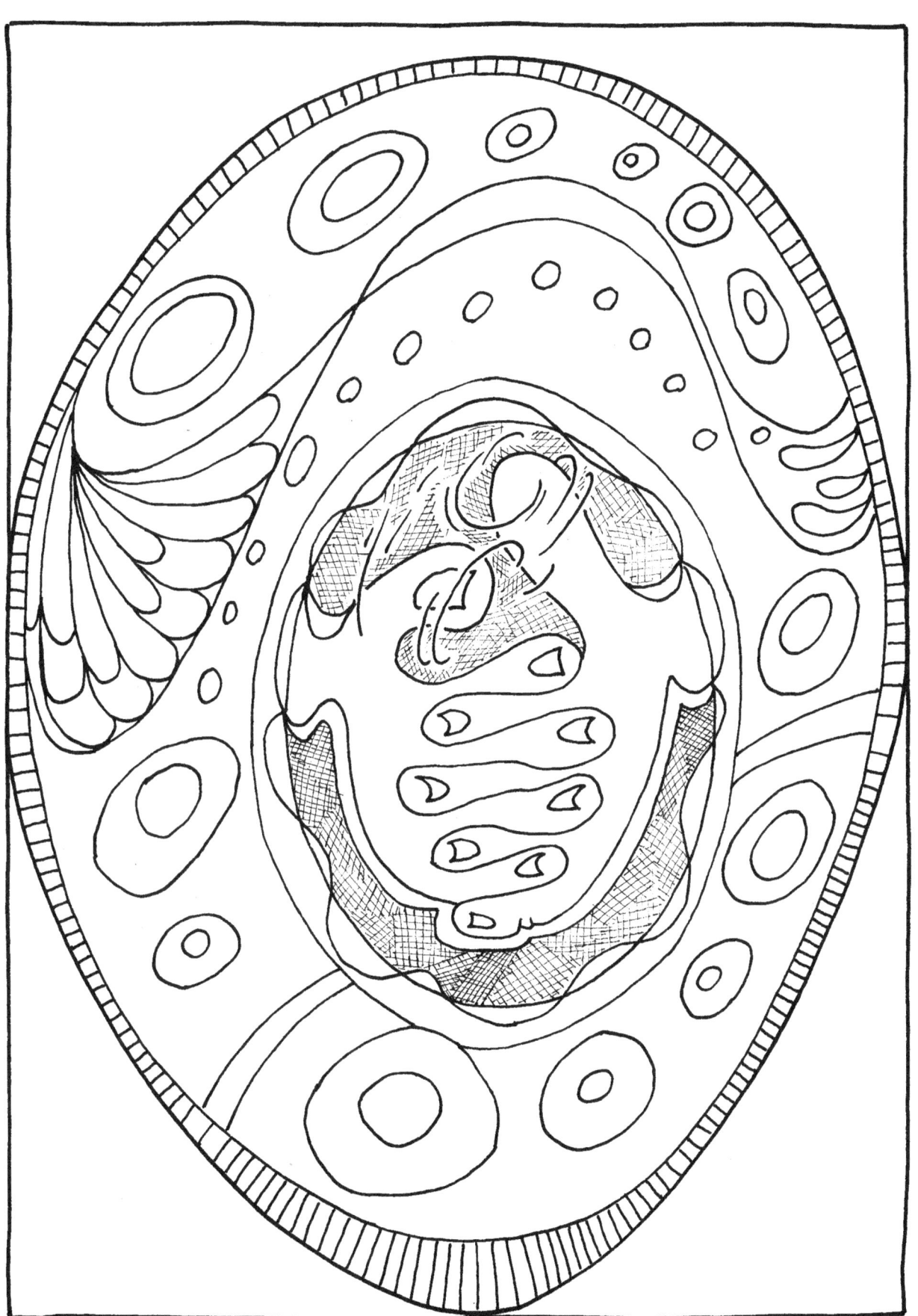

INSIDERS ©2018 Joan Worth De Pere, Wisconsin

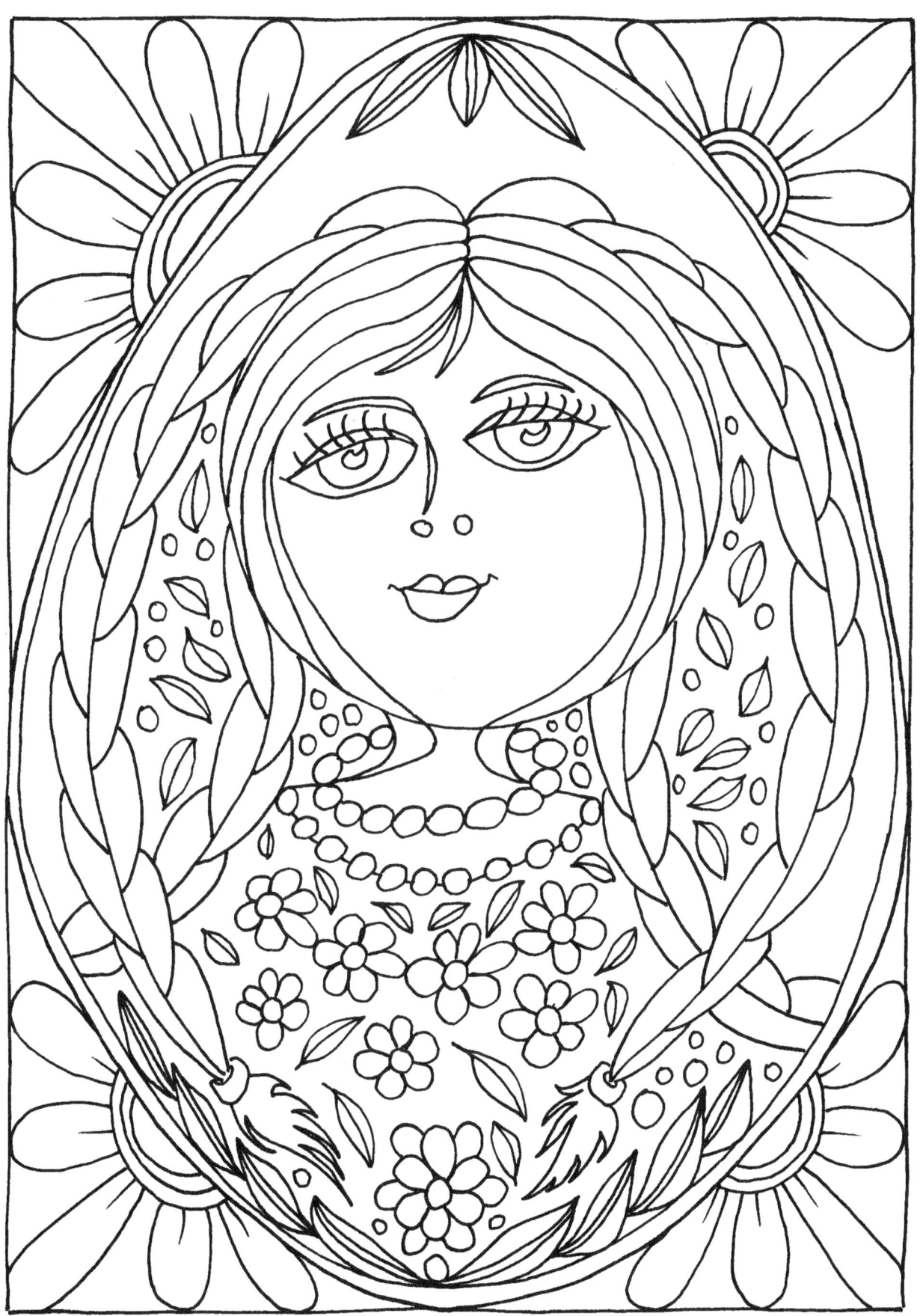

INSIDERS ©2018 Joan Worth De Pere, Wisconsin

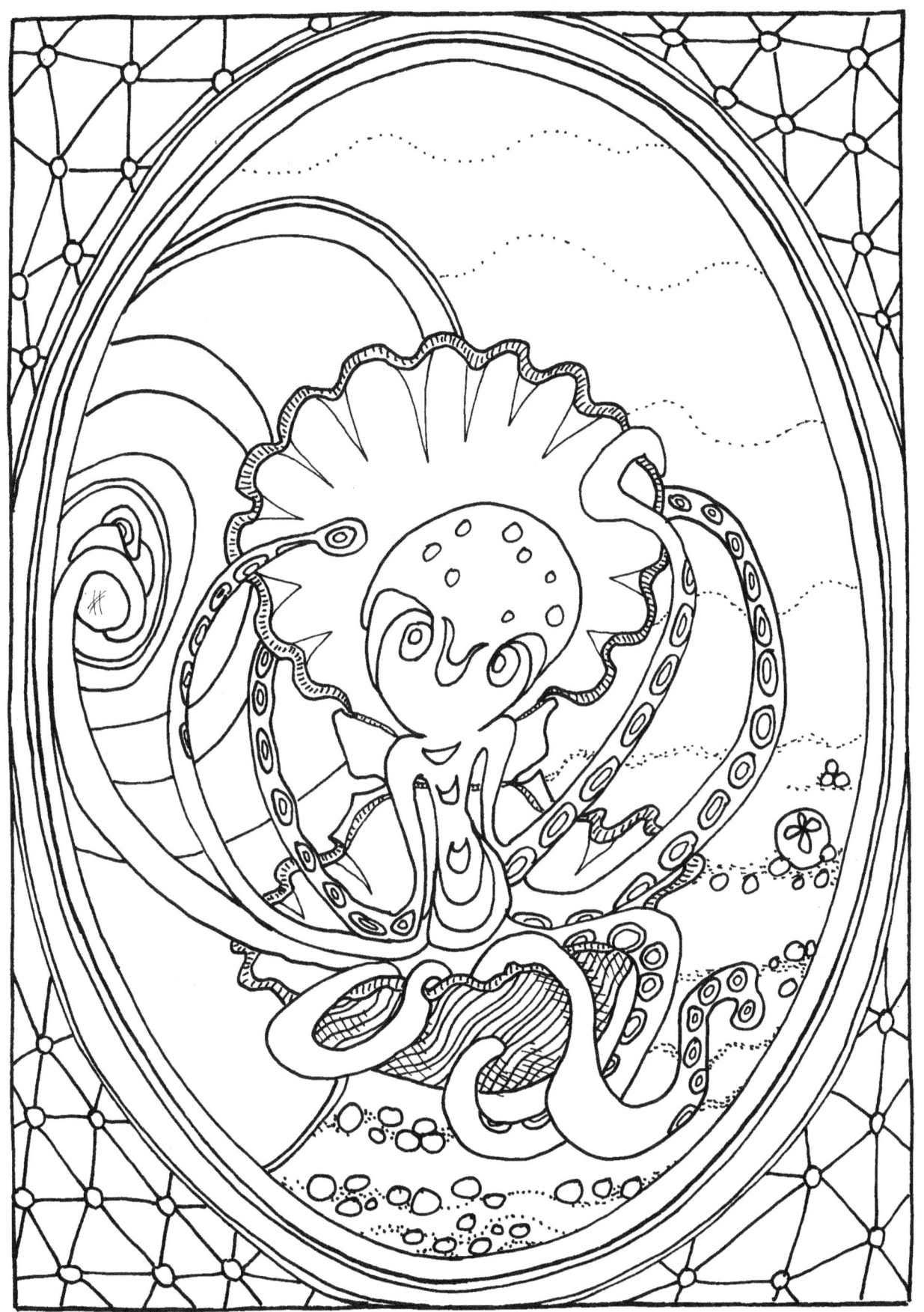

INSIDERS ©2018 Joan Worth De Pere, Wisconsin

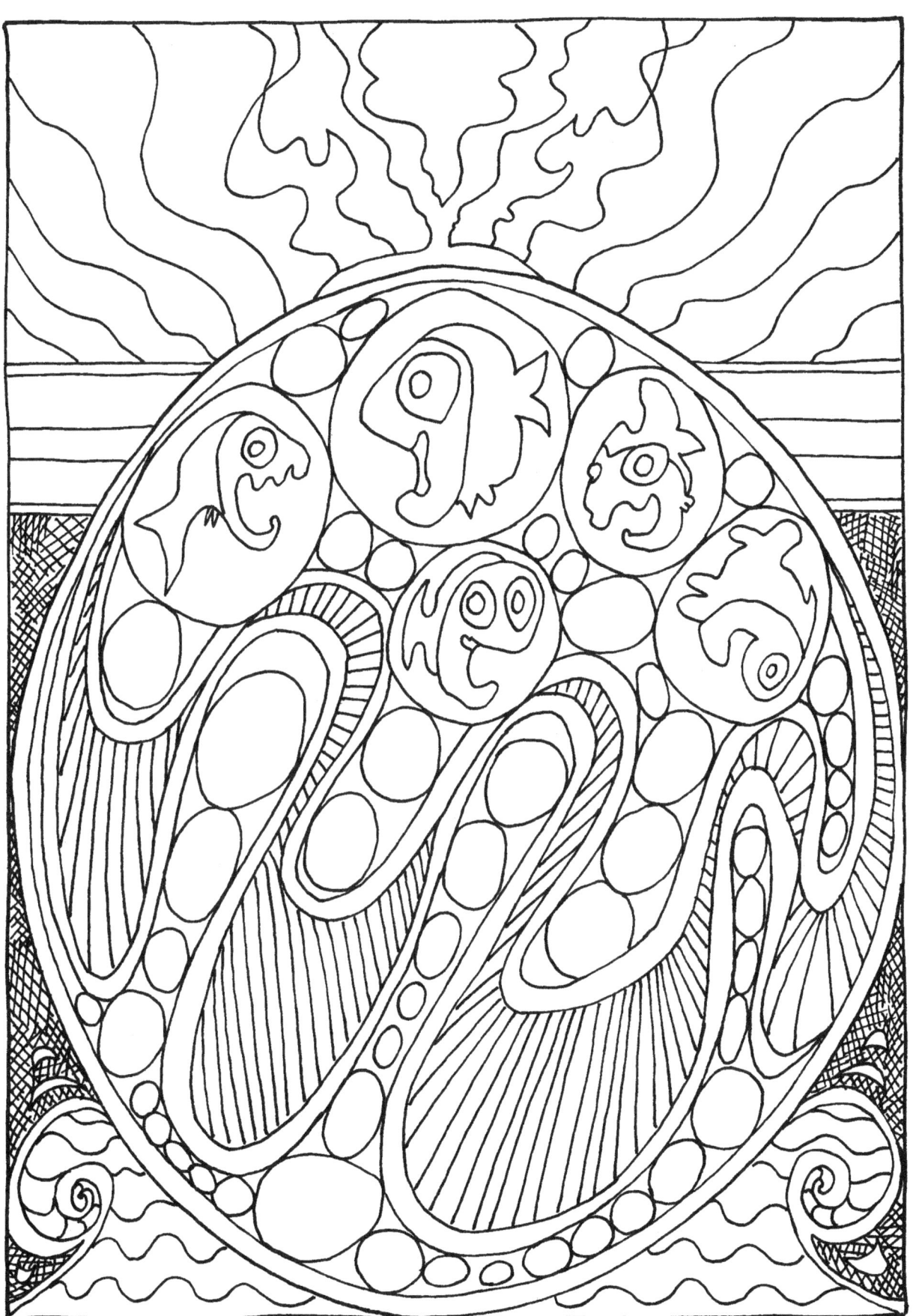

INSIDERS ©2018 Joan Worth De Pere, Wisconsin

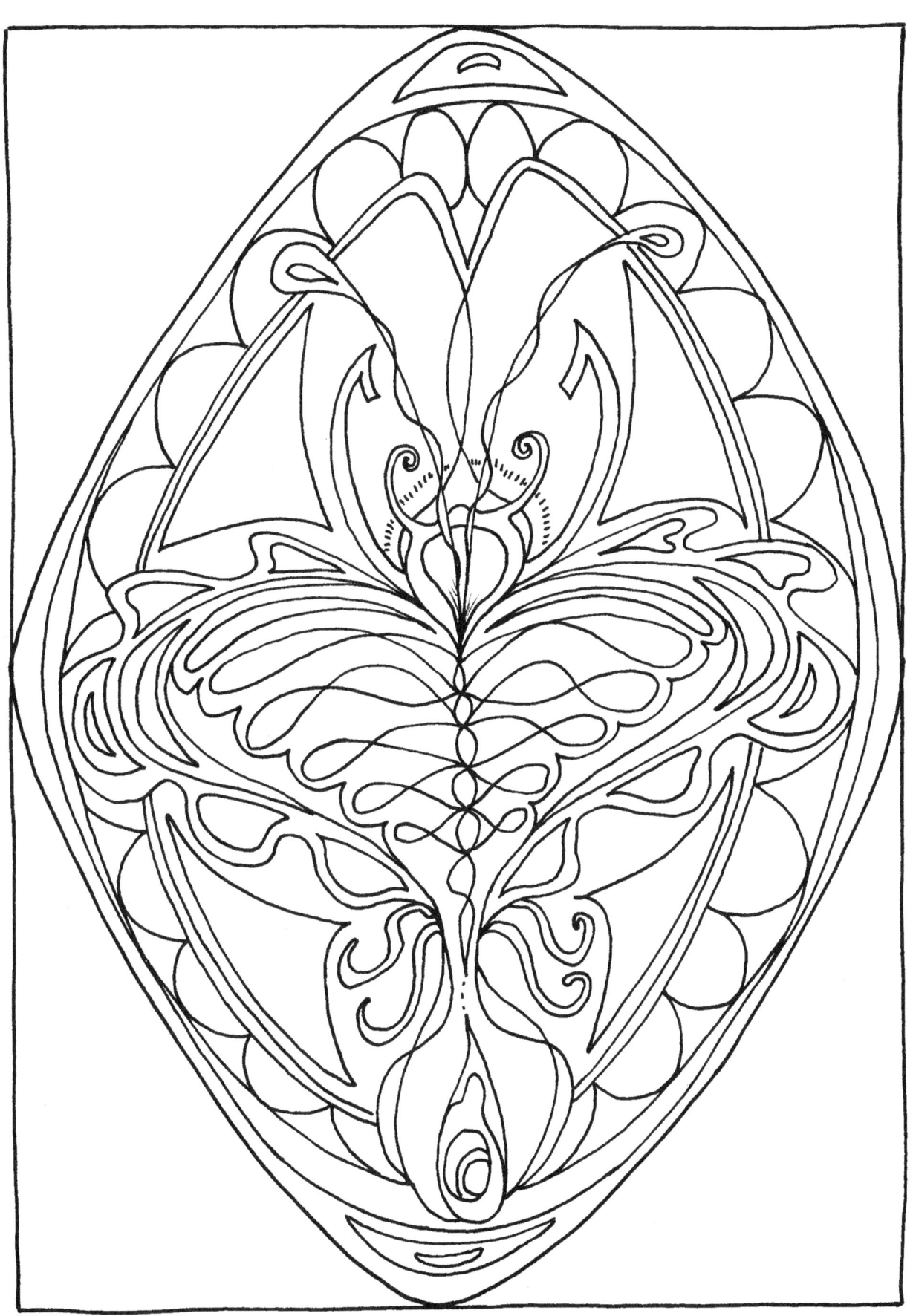

INSIDERS ©2018 Joan Worth De Pere, Wisconsin

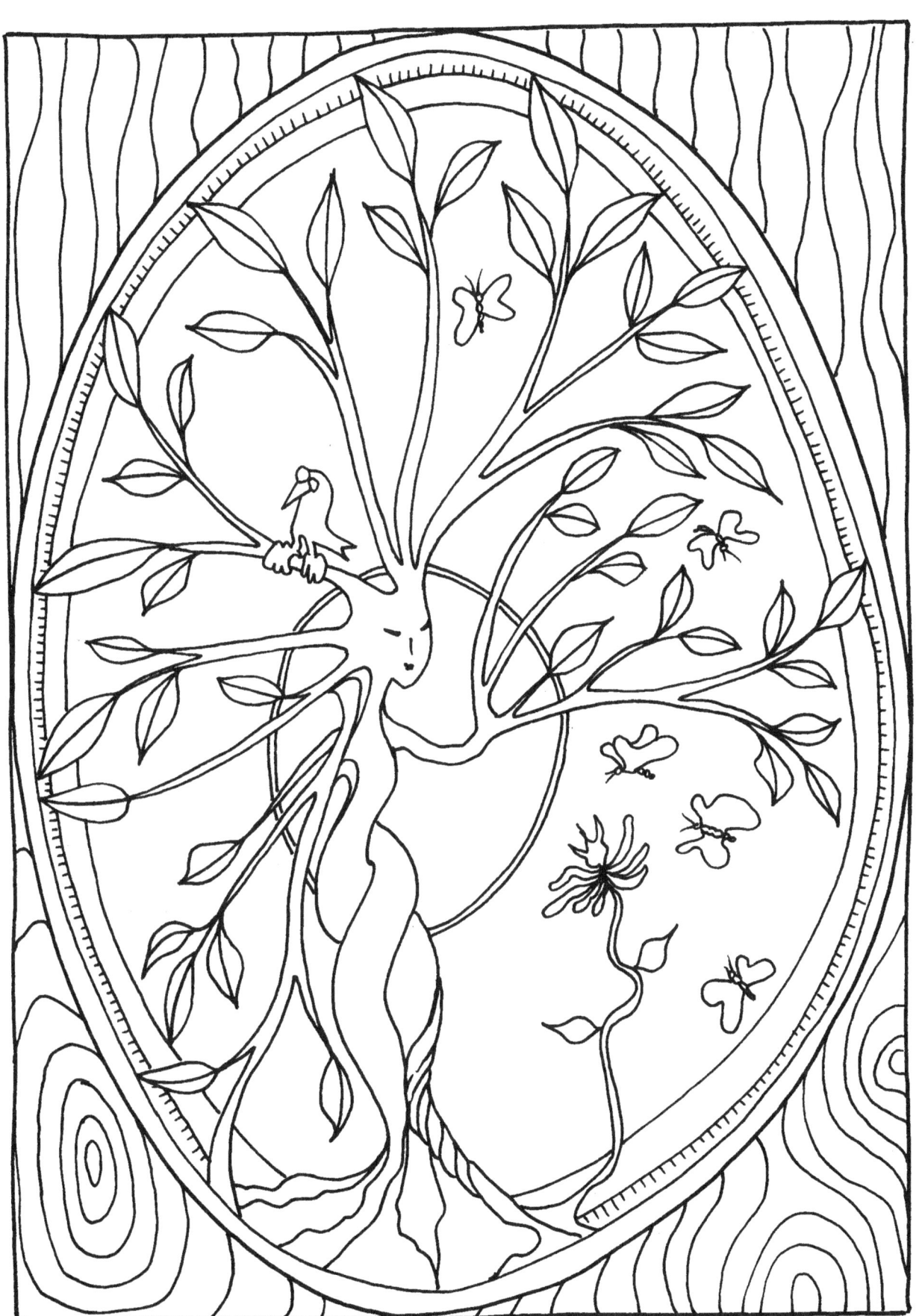

INSIDERS ©2018 Joan Worth De Pere, Wisconsin

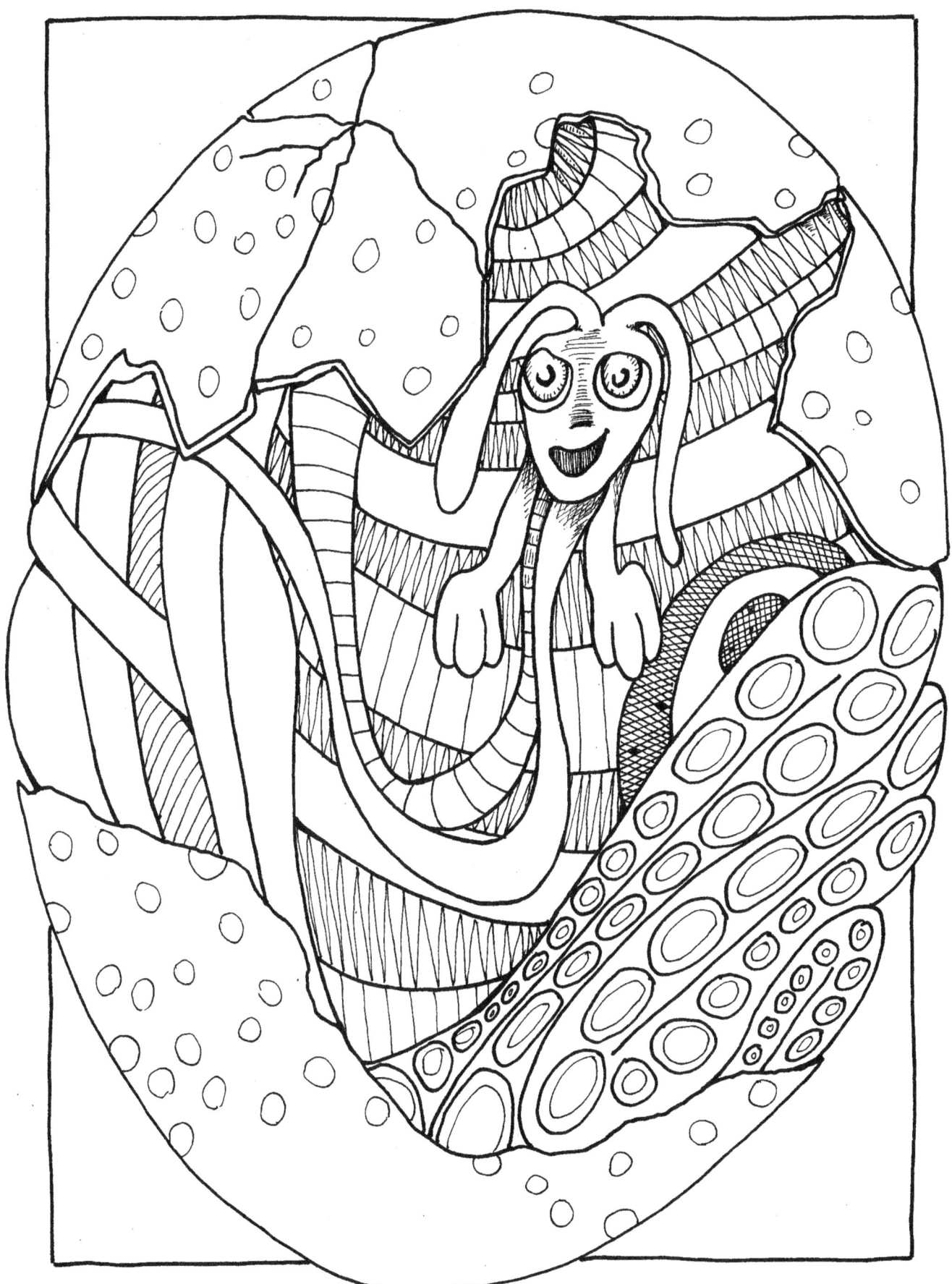

INSIDERS ©2018 Joan Worth De Pere, Wisconsin

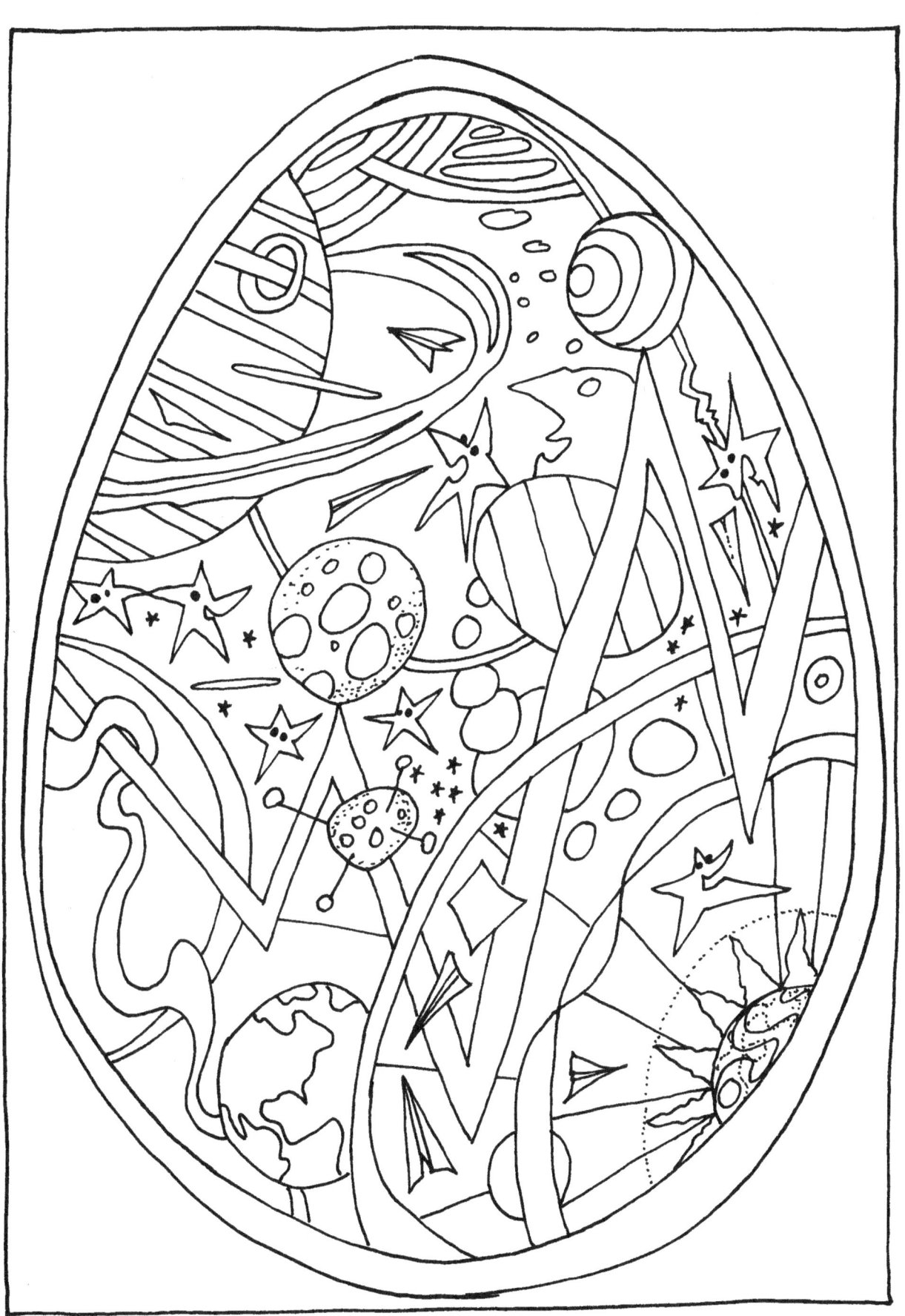

INSIDERS ©2018 Joan Worth De Pere, Wisconsin

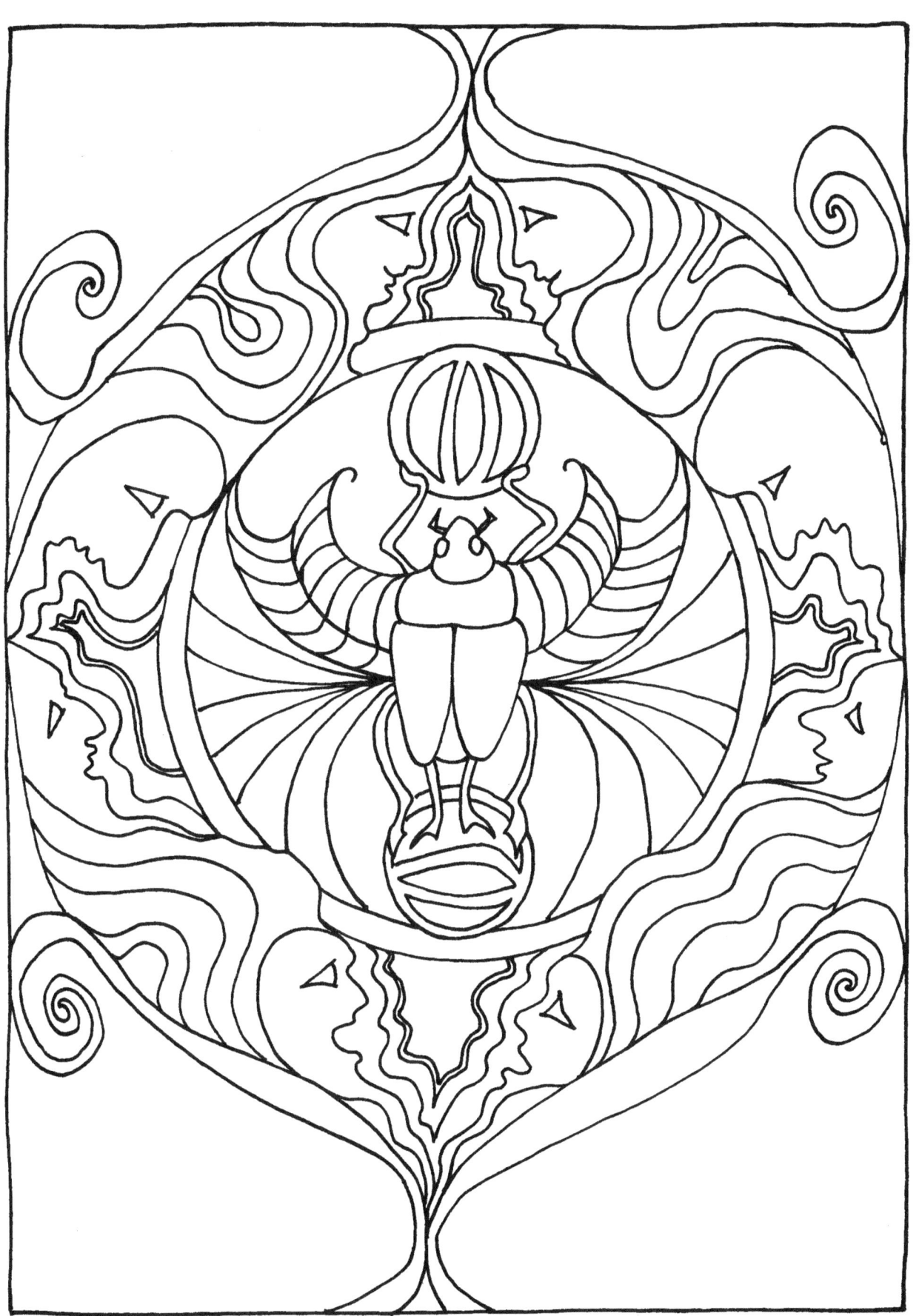

INSIDERS ©2018 Joan Worth De Pere, Wisconsin

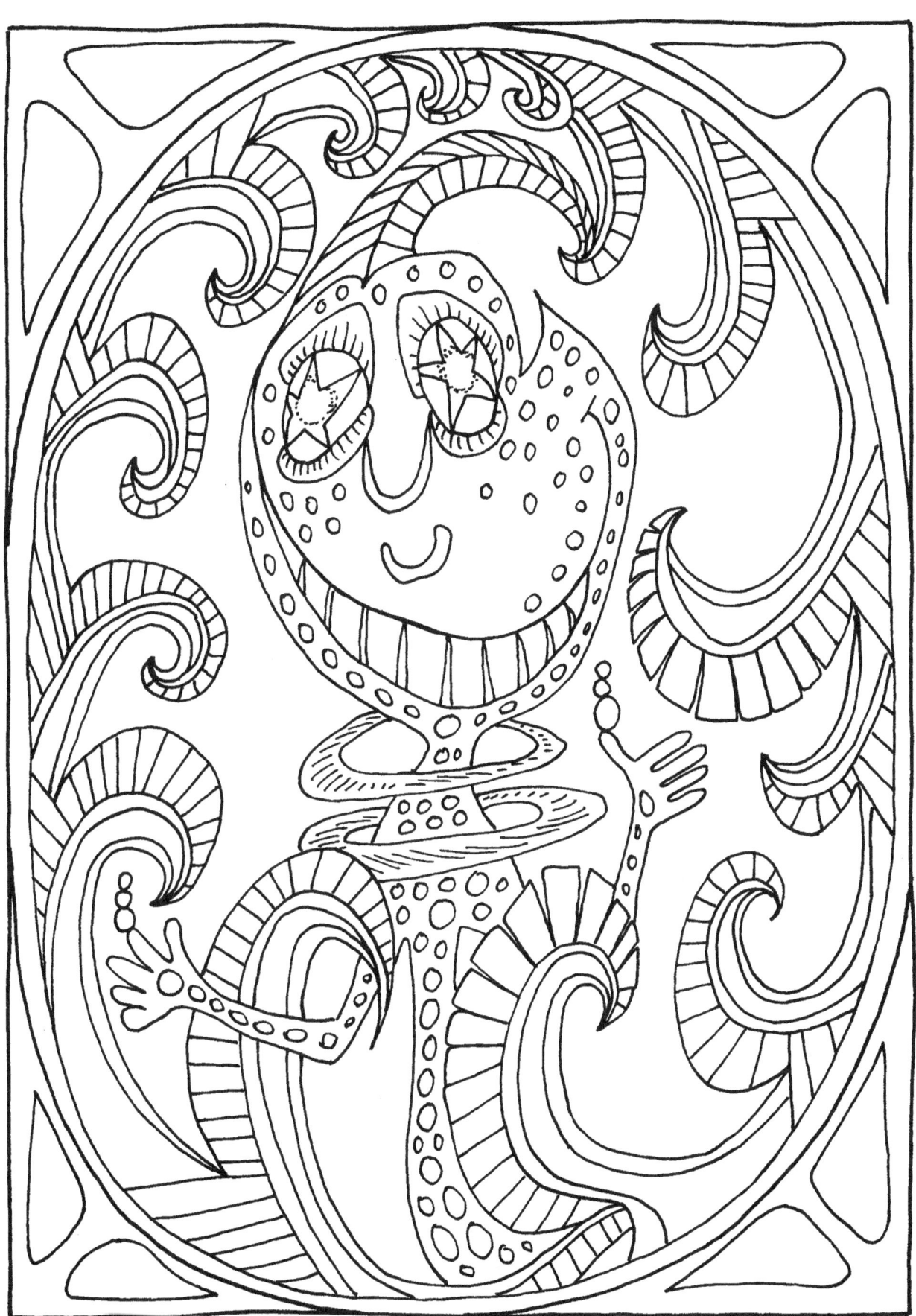

INSIDERS ©2018 Joan Worth De Pere, Wisconsin

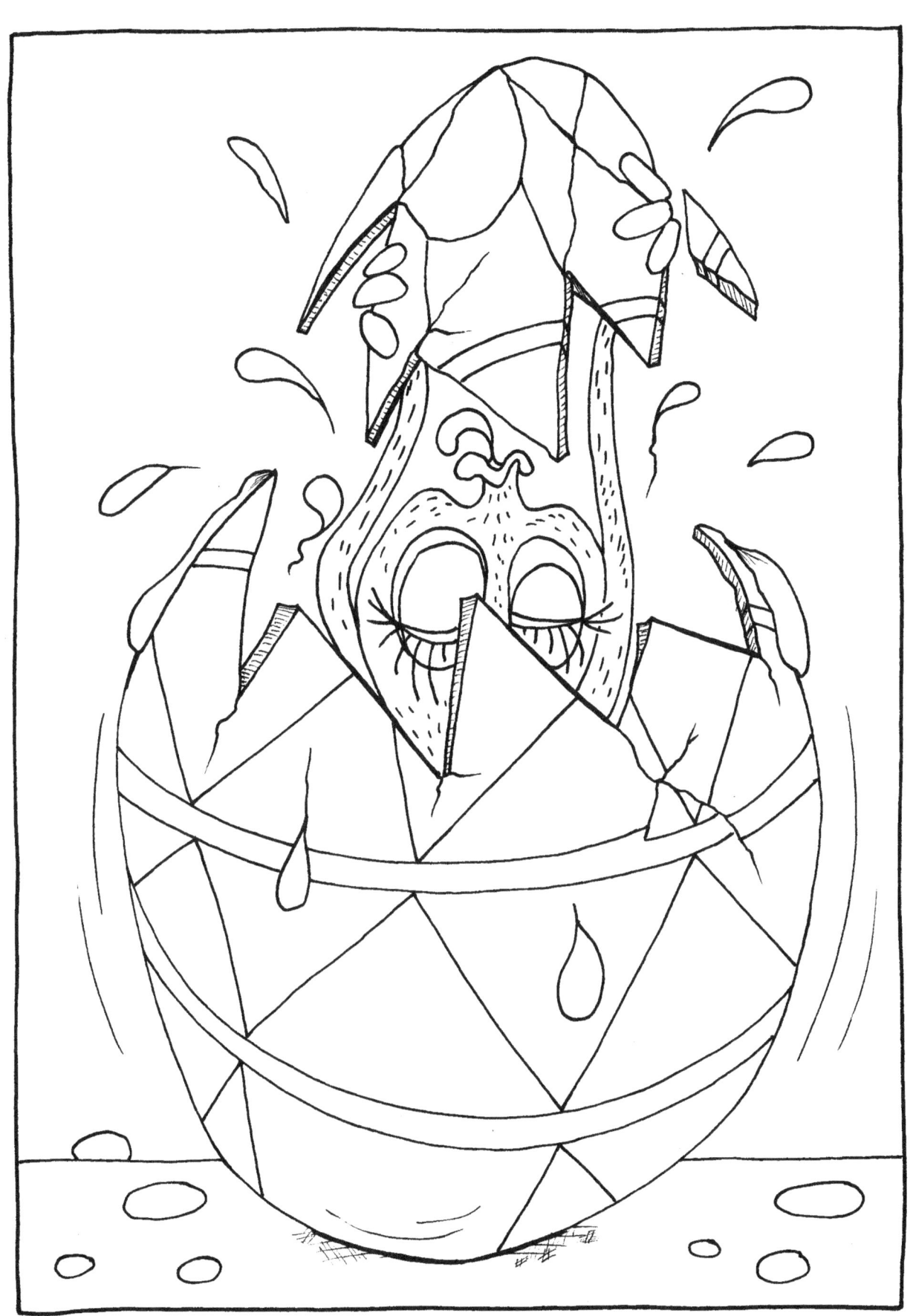

INSIDERS ©2018 Joan Worth De Pere, Wisconsin

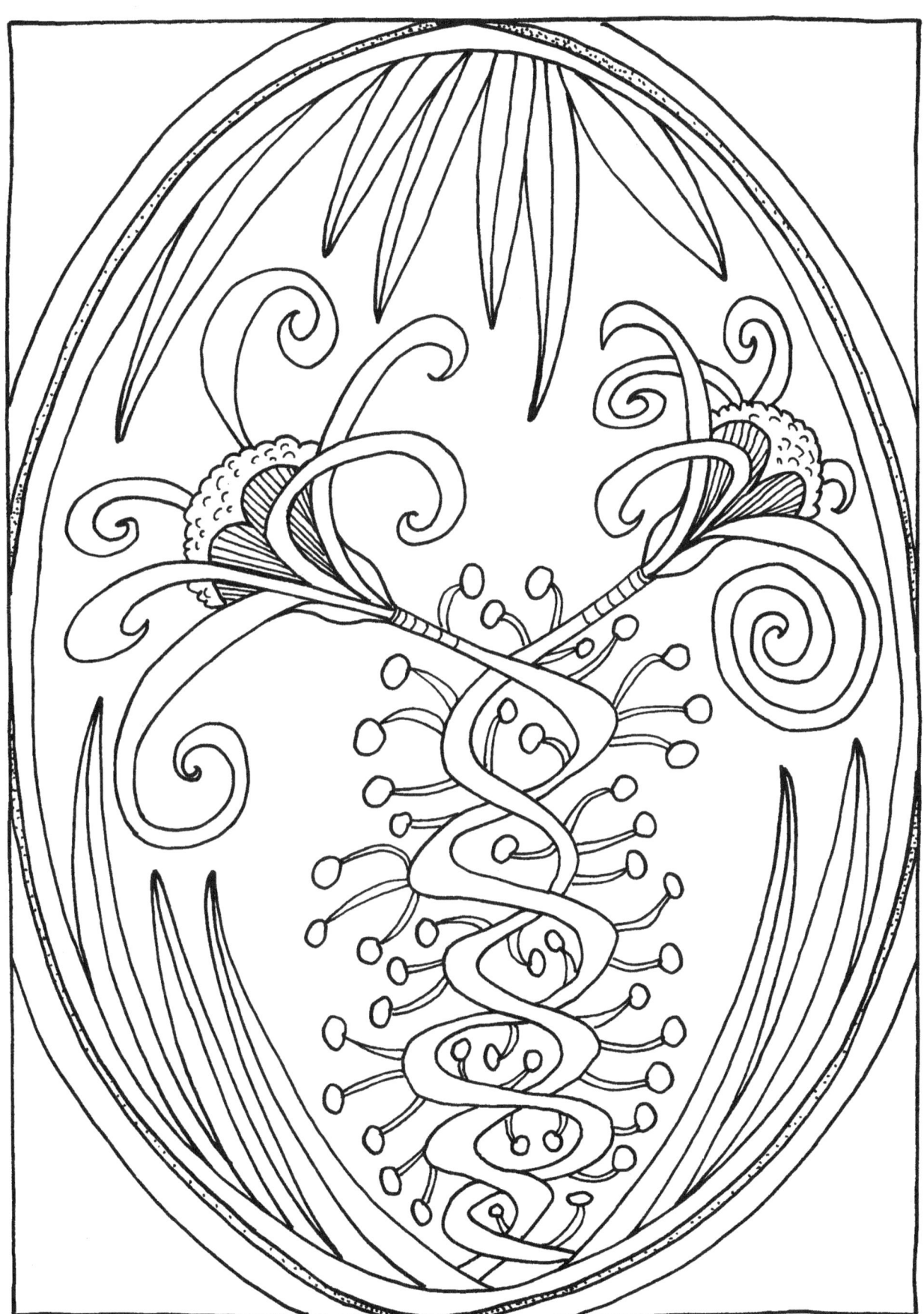

INSIDERS ©2018 Joan Worth De Pere, Wisconsin

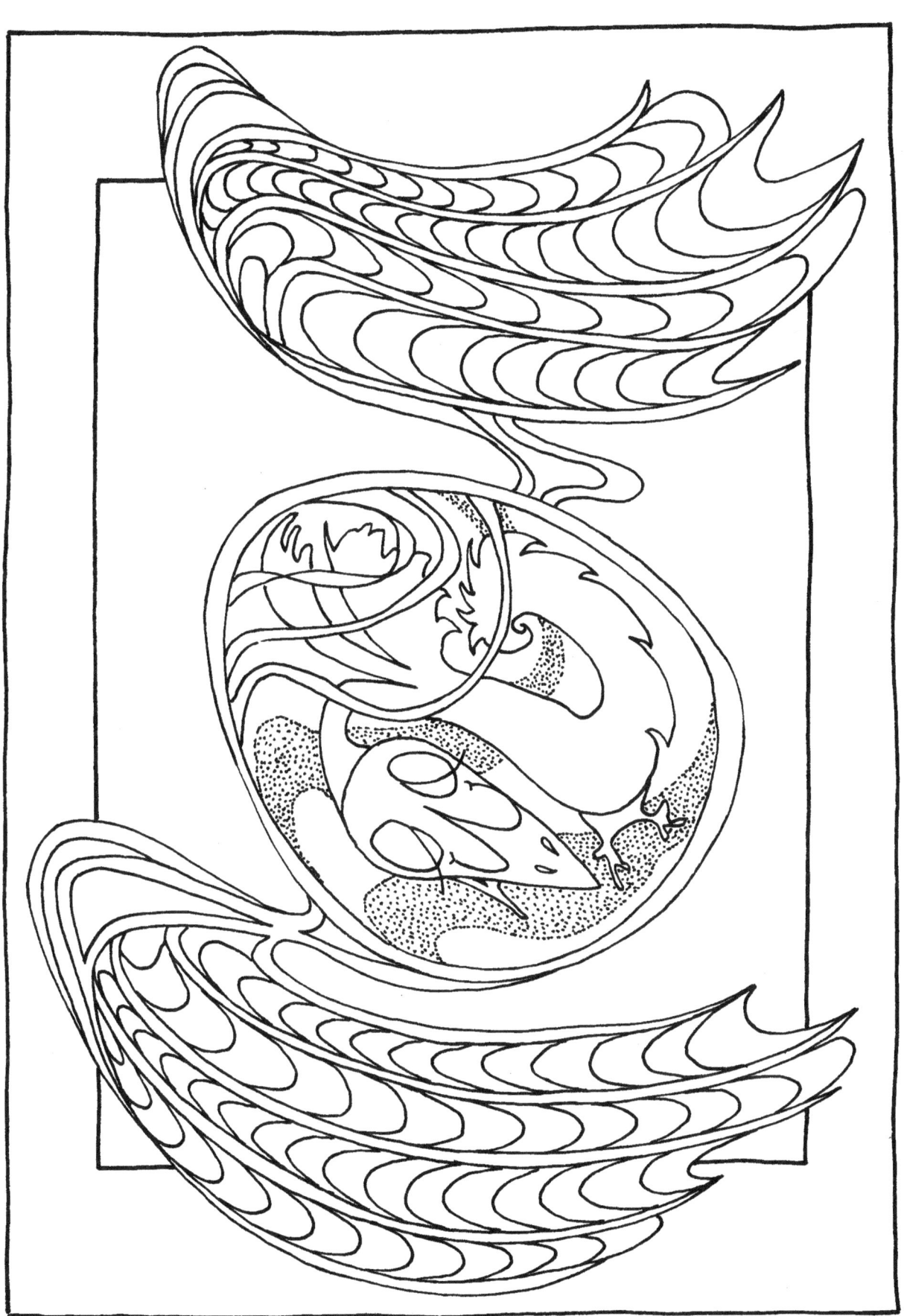

INSIDERS ©2018 Joan Worth De Pere, Wisconsin

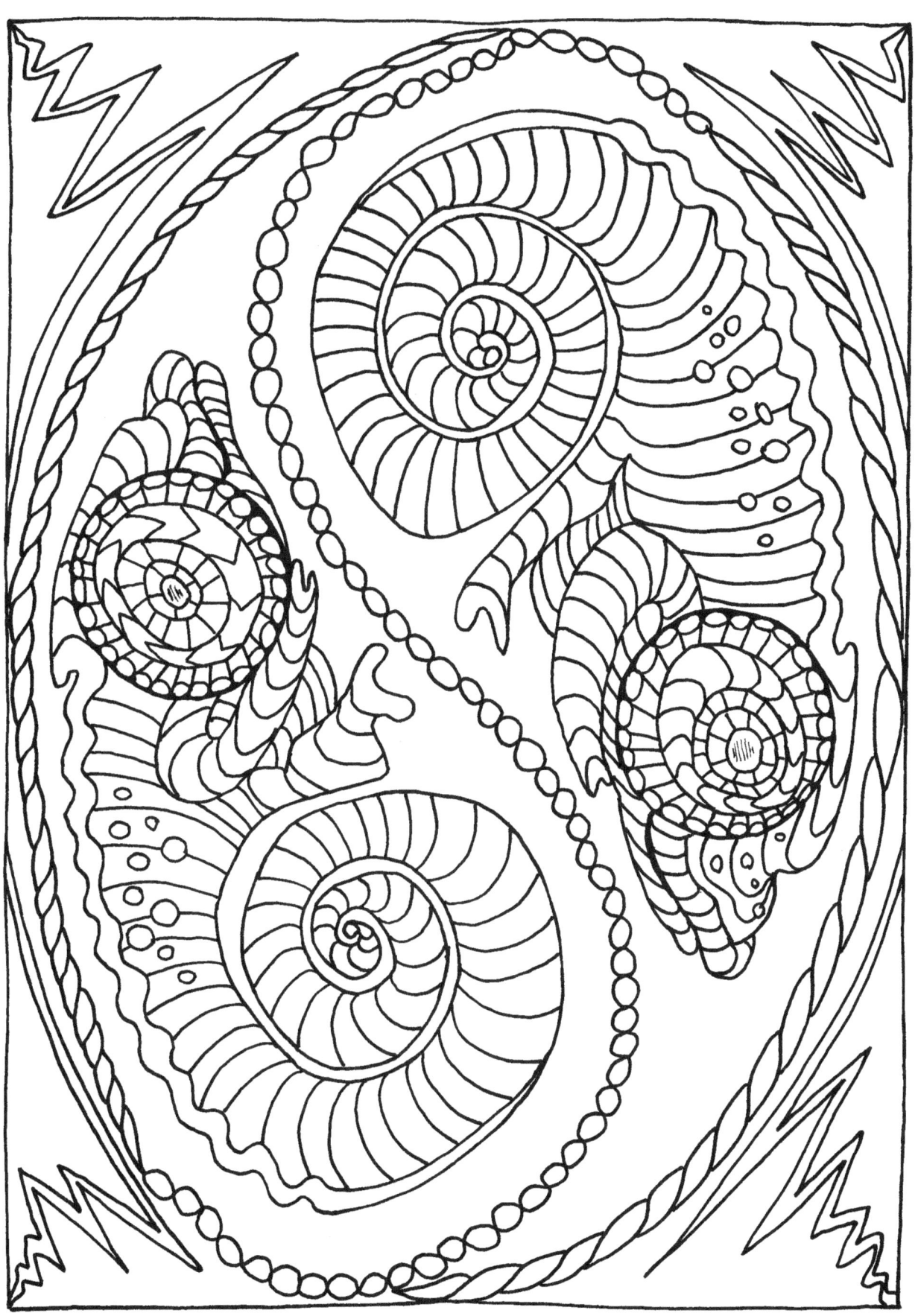

INSIDERS ©2018 Joan Worth De Pere, Wisconsin

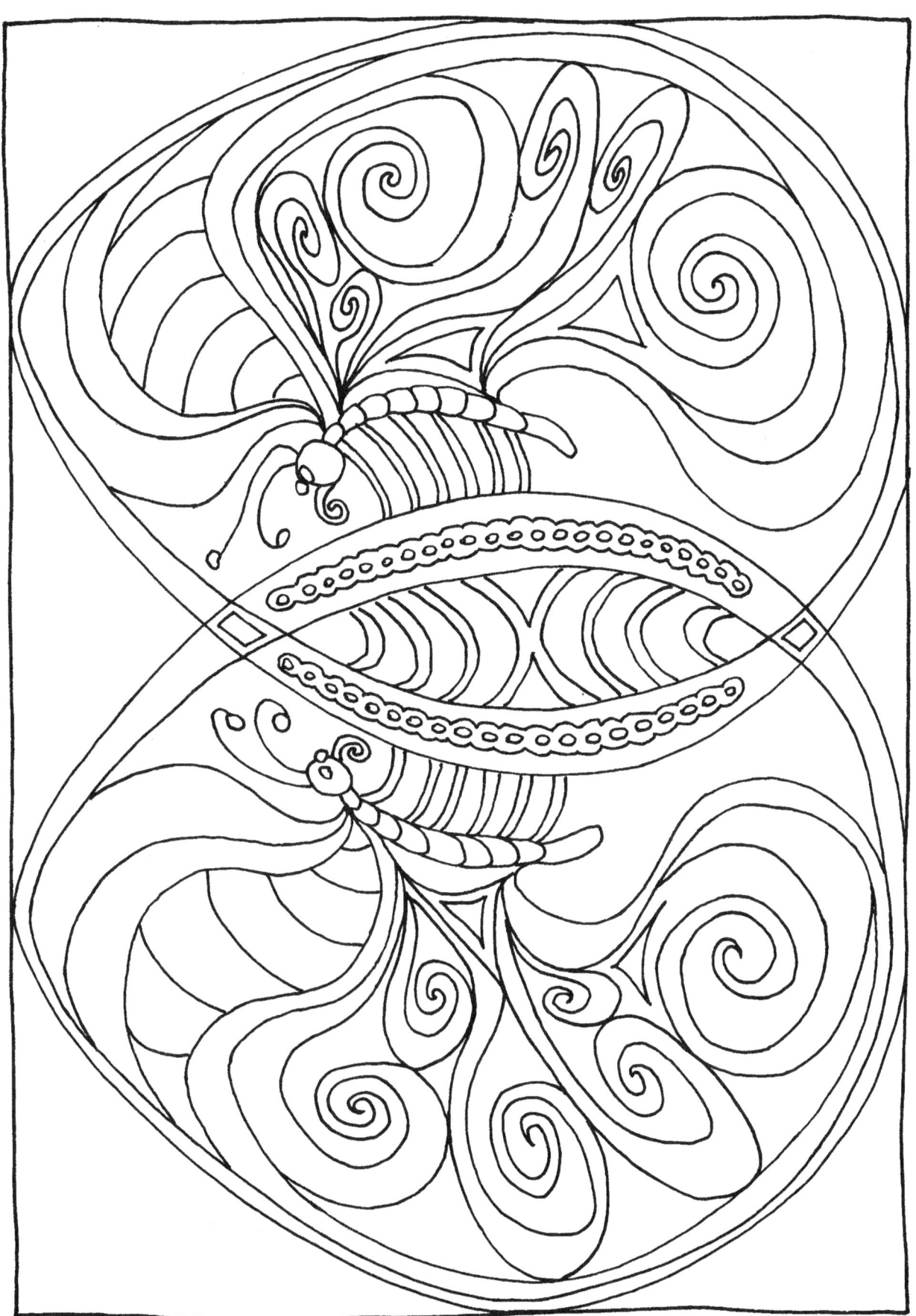

INSIDERS ©2018 Joan Worth De Pere, Wisconsin

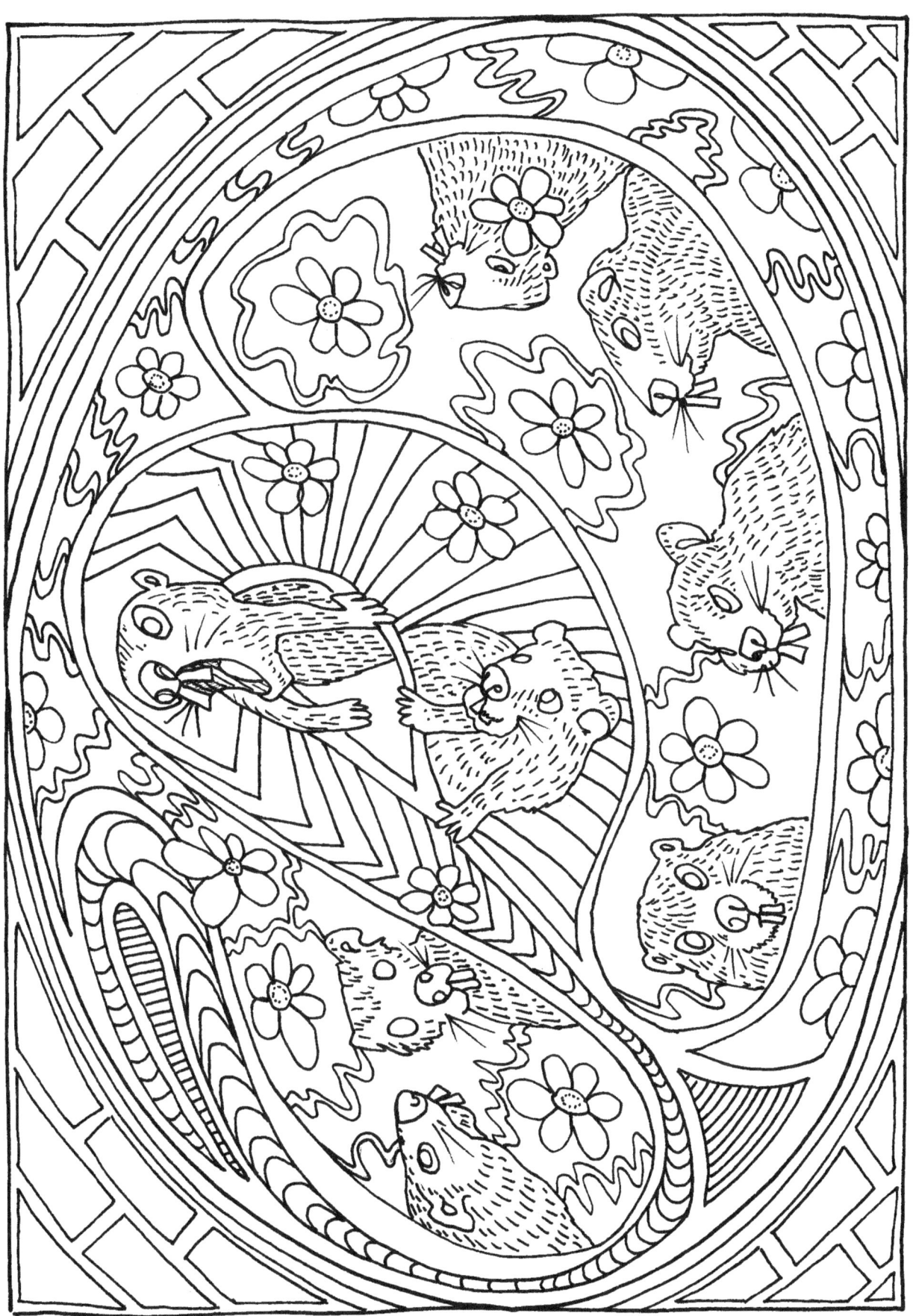

INSIDERS ©2018 Joan Worth De Pere, Wisconsin

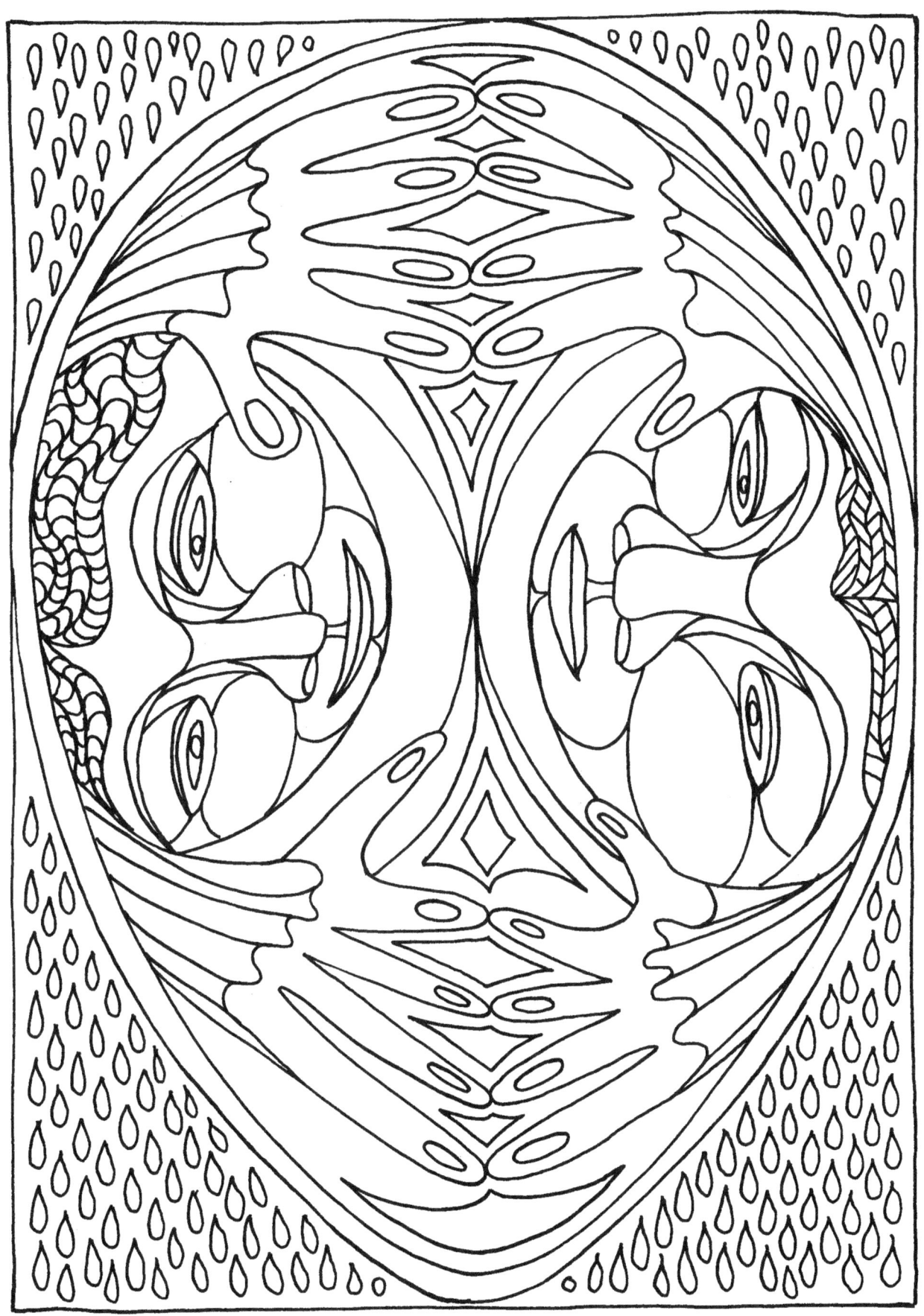

INSIDERS ©2018 Joan Worth De Pere, Wisconsin

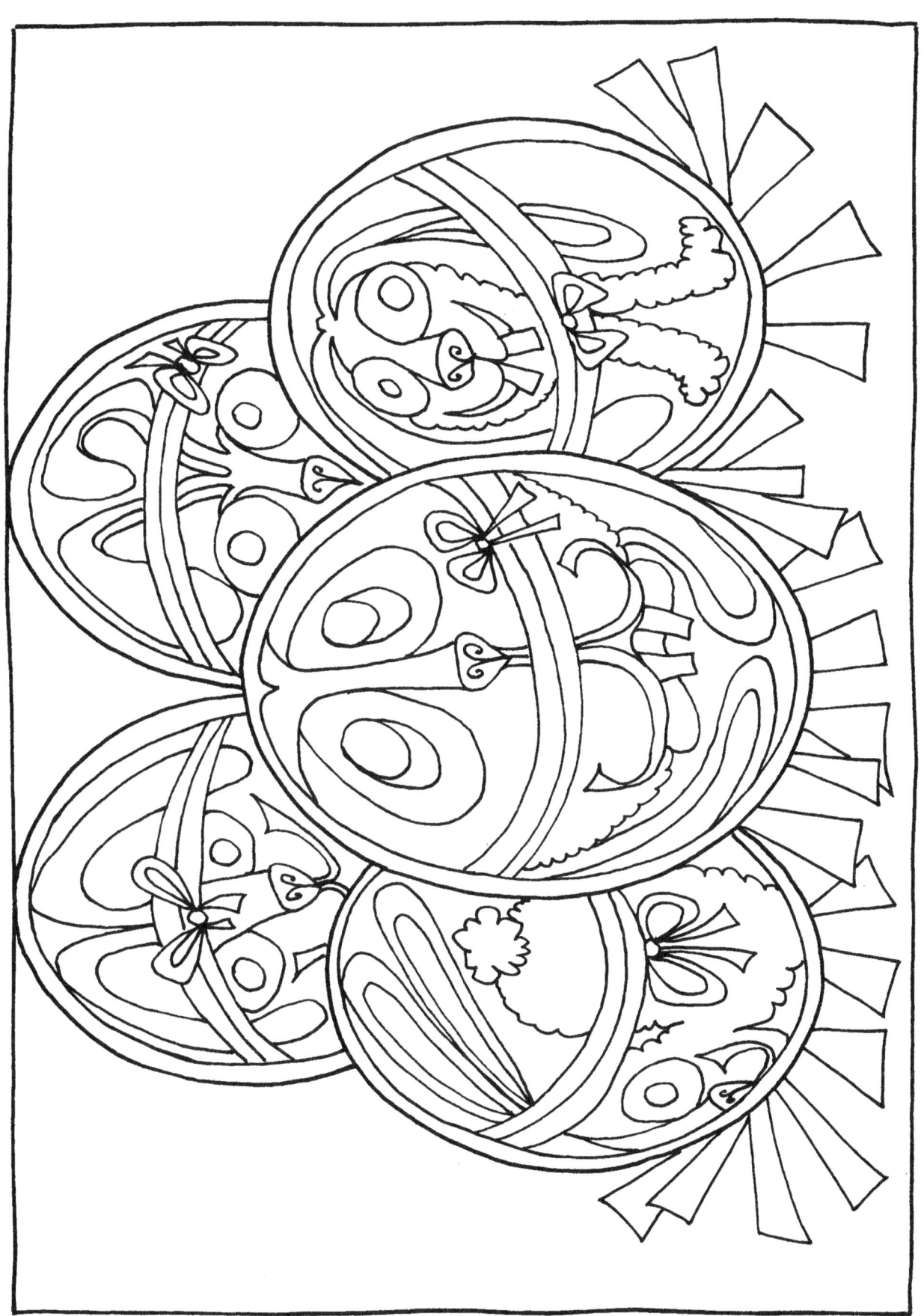

INSIDERS ©2018 Joan Worth De Pere, Wisconsin

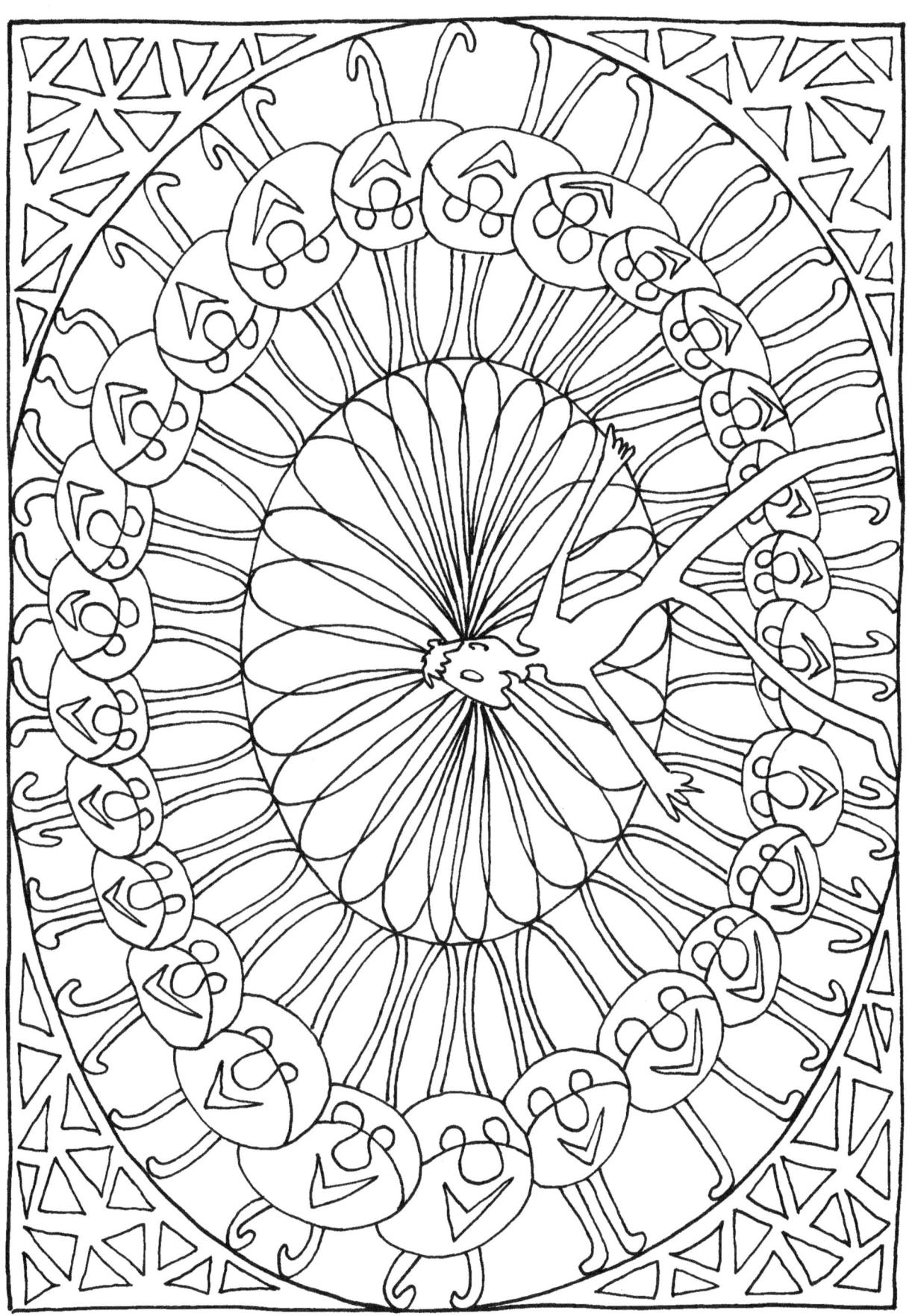

INSIDERS ©2018 Joan Worth De Pere, Wisconsin

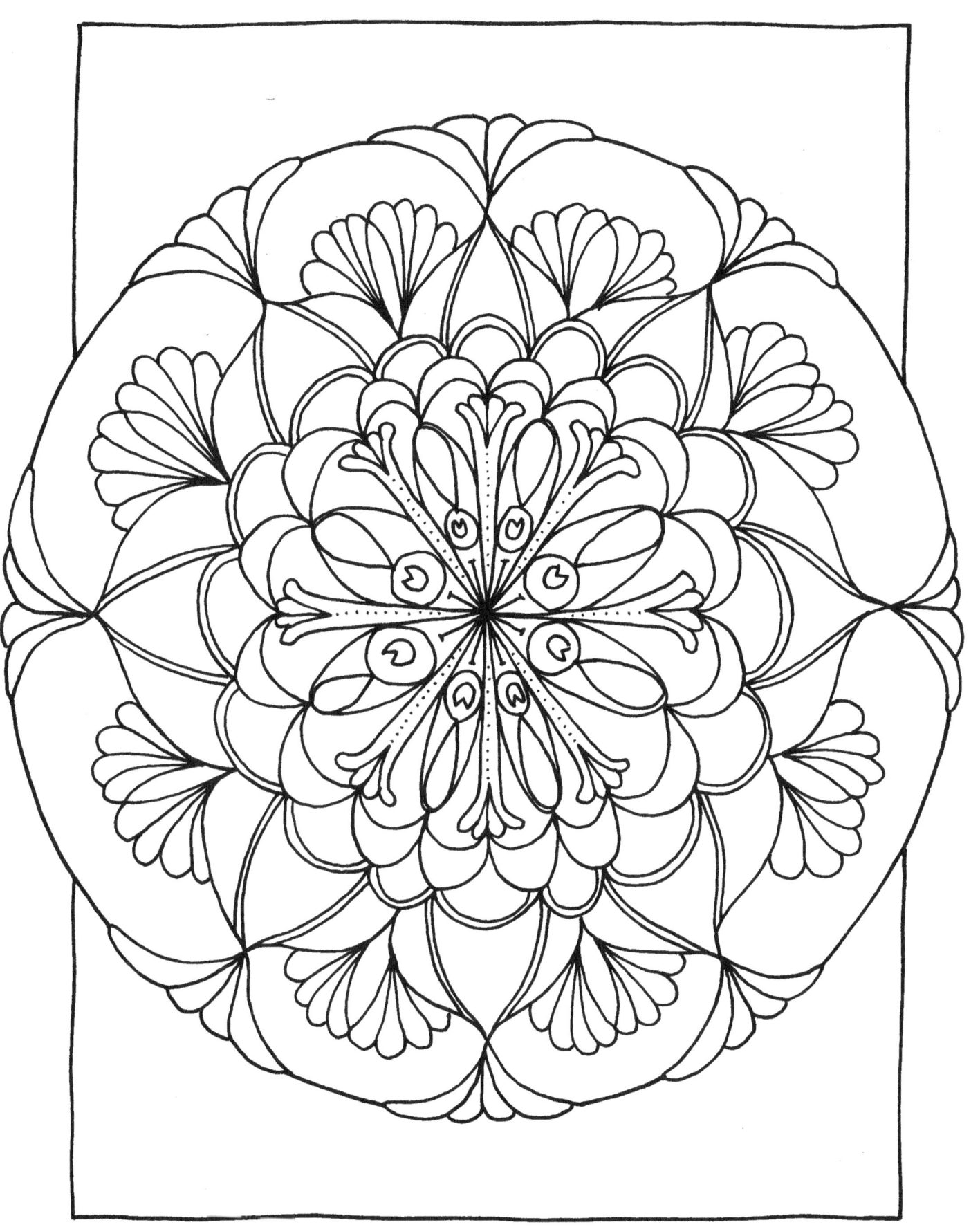

INSIDERS ©2018 Joan Worth De Pere, Wisconsin

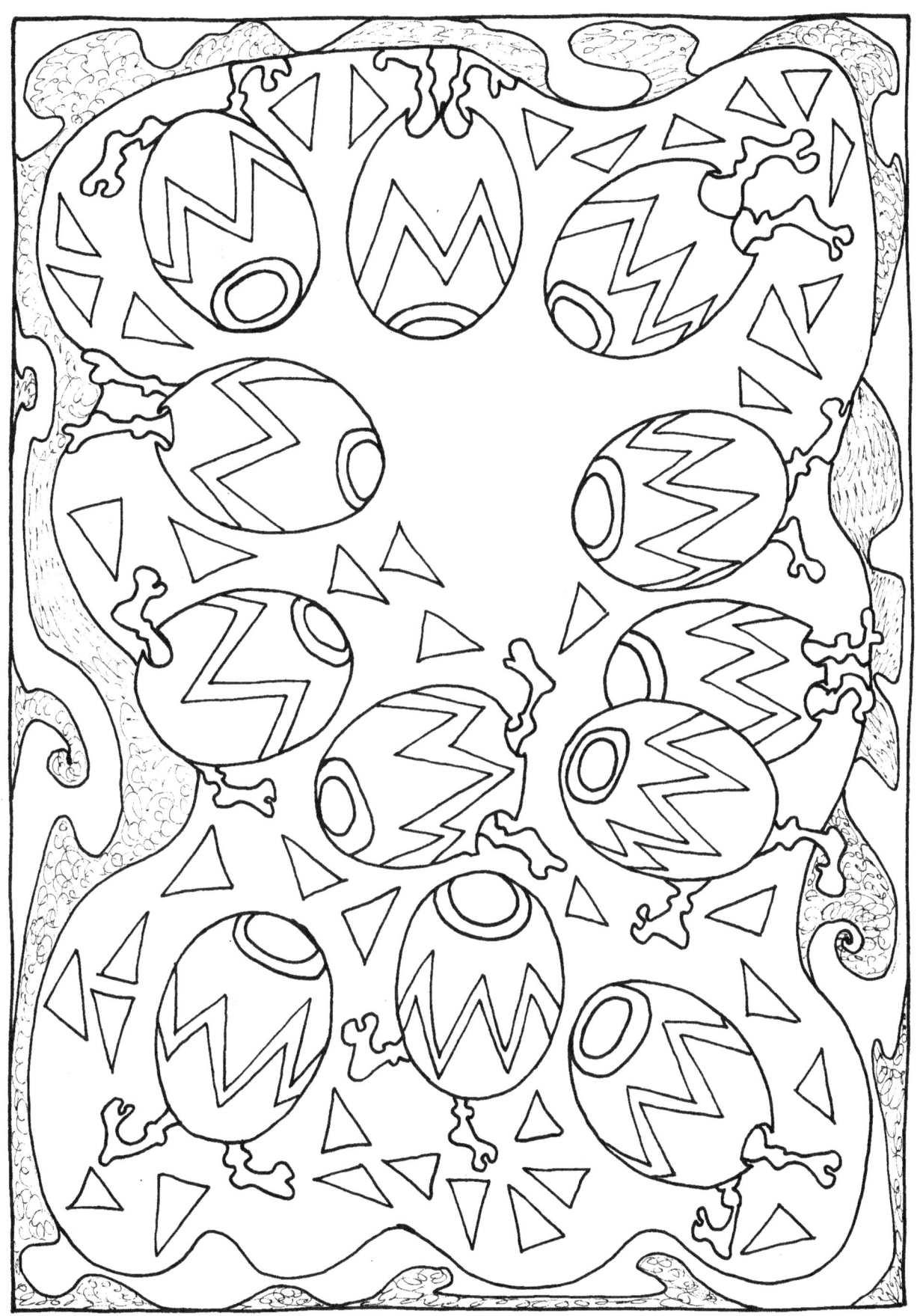

INSIDERS ©2018 Joan Worth De Pere, Wisconsin

www.ingramcontent.com/pod-product-compliance
Lightning Source LLC
Chambersburg PA
CBHW060004230526
45472CB00008B/1938